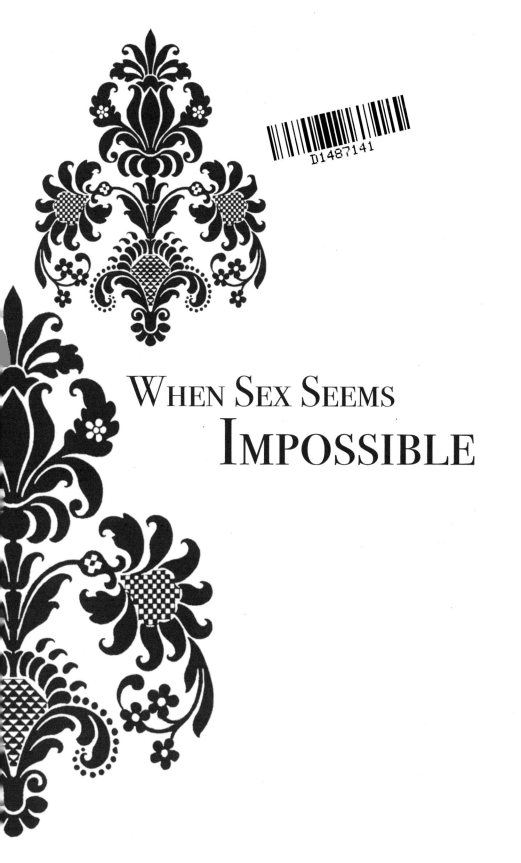

WHEN SEX SEEMS
IMPOSSIBLE

WHEN SEX SEEMS
IMPOSSIBLE

*Stories of Vaginismus &
How You Can Achieve Intimacy*

PETER T. PACIK, MD, FACS
WITH JONI B. COLE

odyne
publishing

Manchester, New Hampshire

Designed and illustrated by Nicole Piar
www.ghostkitten.com

Published in the United States
by Odyne Publishing, Manchester, NH 03104
Printed in the United States of America
First Edition

Library of Congress Control Number: 2010937583

Pacik, Peter T.
    When sex seems impossible: stories of vaginismus and
how you can achieve intimacy / Peter T. Pacik — First Edition
ISBN 978-0-9830134-0-2

For more information about this book or about the author, please contact:

Peter T. Pacik, MD, FACS
Plastic Surgery Professional Association
57 Bay Street, Manchester, NH 03104
phone: (800) 640-0290
e-mail: info@plasticsurgerypa.com
www.plasticsurgerypa.com

A Note to Readers

Part of my vision for writing this book is to tell the story of vaginismus, as told to me by my patients. While each of these women is unique, their stories share similar themes. They are in unconsummated relationships on the verge of unraveling. They are unable to bear children. They have lived for too long with the deep pain, shame, and confusion associated with this condition.

I want vaginismus sufferers to know that they are not alone. I want them to know that health care professionals are committed to learning more about this condition and advocating for their patients. I want them to know that there is a cure.

This book is dedicated to the millions of women who suffer from vaginismus worldwide, and specifically to my patients whose stories and insights have taught me so much, not only about vaginismus, but how to be a better doctor. Your voices deserve to be heard.

Peter T. Pacik, MD, FACS

A Special Thanks

This book, and my practice in general, has benefitted enormously from the insights, dialogue, feedback, spirited exchanges, and ongoing support from members of three invaluable professional organizations to which I belong. These organizations include: the American Association of Sexuality Educators, Counselors and Therapists (AASECT), a non-profit whose diverse members share an interest in promoting understanding of human sexuality and healthy sexual behavior; the International Society for the Study of Women's Health (ISSWH), a multidisciplinary, academic, and scientific organization devoted to communication among scholars, researchers, and practitioners about women's sexual function and sexual experience; and the Society for the Scientific Study of Sexuality (SSSS), an international organization of interdisciplinary professionals dedicated to the advancement of knowledge about sexuality.

CONTENTS

Introduction

STORIES THAT NEED TO BE TOLD

Dear Doctor Pacik....

...I'm desperate. Can you help me? This is my last chance before we get a divorce. We have always wanted a family, and here I am, a freak. I am so embarrassed. I'm tired of crying. PLEASE HELP ME...

...My 21-year-old daughter has what is probably Level 5 vaginismus. She has not been able to have a physical exam of any kind, can't use tampons, and cannot have sexual intercourse. She went to physical therapy on a weekly basis for about a year, trying to use dilators and biofeedback, and made virtually no progress. The therapist finally gave up on her...

...My wife was already in contact with you two years ago and I was scared of letting her perform the procedure. Now, two years later, I realize this may be the solution to help cure her vaginismus so I'm ready to set up an appointment...

...I just want a normal marriage, a family, to feel like a normal woman. I can't take another doctor telling me there is nothing left to do, that I have no other option. I feel like this has stopped my whole life and I'm trapped. I've hurt the one I love most and I can't fix it. Please help me. I don't know what else to do...

...I cannot tell you how relieved I am to know that there is still some hope for me. I have been practicing insertion with dilators for some time, but not with much benefit. My eight-year relationship is almost on the verge of break-up because of this...

Welcome to my inbox. Every week I receive e-mails from women who can't have intercourse or any kind of vaginal penetration due to pain and fear. Some of this correspondence comes from young women just starting out in their sexual lives. Other messages are from women well past their child-bearing years. Sometimes their husbands or mothers contact me on their behalf. Some of these women feel like "freaks." They are worried about their relationships. They just want to be "normal."

By now I have read hundreds of e-mails similar to the ones shared here, yet the suffering in them is so palpable that each new inquiry still tugs at my heart. Many of these women have already been to several doctors, therapists, and even specialists. Some of them have been given a diagnosis, but the treatments they have tried, be it surgeries, years of talk or physical therapy, working with dilators on their own, have not worked. Others have never been given a name for what is wrong with them. They have no idea why every attempt at intercourse or vaginal penetration fills them with pain and panic.

In the process of seeking help for their problem, many of these women have been told, "It's all in your head." They have been called "frigid" and accused of not loving men, including their husbands. In their search for answers, they are often left to their own devices. Many of them have found advice and community on the Internet, but also misinformation.

Understandably, most of the women who contact me because they can't have intercourse are nervous about consulting with yet another doctor and trying a relatively new treatment program. They wonder, *Will I be wasting more time, money, and emotional energy?* Still, they refuse to give up, even if it means travelling across the country or to another country for help.

A Condition with a Long History... and a New Treatment

What most of these women have is a condition called vaginismus, a "sexual pain disorder" in which muscles in the vagina clench involuntarily because of extreme fear of the pain or anticipated pain of vaginal penetration. *The first night we tried to have sex it was IMPOSSIBLE! I began to get anxious. I couldn't breathe. It felt like he was trying to break a wall down...*

Most of the general public has never even heard of vaginismus, and indeed many gynecologists and sex therapists are also unfamiliar with the condition, but vaginismus is not that uncommon. Researchers estimate that from 1 to 7 percent of the female population worldwide suffer from vaginismus. And it has afflicted women for centuries. In fact, the first written reference to what was likely vaginismus appeared in 1547 in a scientific work called *Women's Diseases* by Trotula di Ruggiero of Salerno, Italy. Considered the first gynecologist and a pioneer in women's health, Trotula wrote in an early publication, "It is such a contraction in the genital region that even a seduced woman can be a virgin."

My own involvement with vaginismus started in 2005 when a patient wrote to me asking if I could treat her vaginismus with Botox, a purified neurotoxin used in medicine as a muscle relaxant. In researching her own symptoms, she had found a reference to a promising early study that suggested Botox might also be an effective way to treat vaginismus.

I have been a practicing plastic surgeon since 1972, and have delivered thousands of Botox injections to erase frown lines, but I knew nothing about the drug's application for this condition. In truth, I had never heard of vaginismus. It was only after months of research, and with some trepidation that I eventually agreed to treat this patient with Botox injections to her vaginal muscles. The physician's oath, Above all, do no harm, was a constant refrain in my mind. The outcome was successful, and the patient was able to have pain-free intercourse within a few months.

Since that time, I have continued to develop and refine a compre-hensive treatment protocol for vaginismus, with Botox being just one facet of the program, along with dilation under anesthesia and counseling. Almost all of my vaginismus patients have the most severe level of this complex condition, although most of them are able to progress to intercourse within two weeks to two months. To date, I have had a consistent success rate of over 90 percent, with success measured as pain-free intercourse, or progression to the two largest dilators for women who do not have partners or functioning partners.

When Sex Seems Impossible was inspired by my vaginismus patients who have spent years, sometimes even decades, pursuing treatment for this condition. Just last week I received an inquiry from a prospective new patient who has been working with her dilator kit for three years. She wrote that the process of inserting a dilator still takes at least an hour of trying and copious amounts of lubricant. Her progress to date allows her to now insert a small tampon. I have read so many accounts like this, and feel equal parts admiration and frustration. Three years! This woman deserves to see considerably more progress in such a length of time.

Since treating my first vaginismus patient in 2005, I have made no secret about my own determination to help women overcome this condition. I have started clinical trials. I have written articles. I have joined professional organizations to benefit from the expertise of others and shared thinking. "Why don't you write a book about vaginismus?" several of my patients and associates have asked me over the course of these past five years. Women need information to counter all the myths, misdiagnoses, and misunderstandings surrounding this condition. They need an advocate among the medical community. They need hope.

This book shares what I have learned to date about vaginismus and how to effectively treat it. It is grounded in research, clinical experience, and documented outcomes. But along with the science of vaginismus, I felt it was just as important to tell the stories of vaginismus. At the heart of this book are patient narratives and testimonials that speak to how difficult, even devastating this condition can be, not only for women, but also their partners who love them. Included here are stories of struggle, but also of triumph, as women overcome vaginismus to achieve intercourse and intimacy. These are stories that need to be told.

This book shares the information that I have learned using Botox to treat vaginismus, but it is not intended to denigrate other treatment options. I have had the good fortune to work with a number of medical providers who have dedicated a significant portion of their careers to successfully treating vaginismus. It is simply my desire for this book to be used as one more resource in educating patients and clinicians.

To my readers with vaginismus, or who suspect they may have this condition, I hope this book empowers you in your search for treatment. To my colleagues in the medical community, I hope the information and the powerful stories within these pages motivate you to further your own understanding of this condition. Far more research and shared learning is merited to successfully address this complex condition.

For anyone wanting to know more about the treatment program of vaginismus as described in these pages, my in-box is always open.

Sincerely,
Peter Pacik, MD, FACS

* The case histories, quotes, anecdotes, and outcomes in this book are true. However, names, locations, and other identifying material have been changed to protect the identity of the subjects. Similarities in names or other physically descriptive characteristics between any of the subjects of this book and any other person is purely coincidental.

IT HAS A NAME: VAGINISMUS

Wedding Bell Blues...
and Other Fearful Firsts

On a hot, Southern California evening in July, 1983, Theresa discovered that she couldn't have sex. It happened to be her wedding night. Hours earlier, the 26-year-old brunette had married the man of her dreams. They'd met at a dance and dated for just four months, but despite the quick courtship she knew that Bryan was the one. "He was fun, intelligent, kind," Theresa explained. "My dad always said, 'Watch the guy. If he treats his mother well, he'll treat you well, too.' Bryan is thoughtful," she said with a smile that could be heard in her voice. "Everybody likes him. I'm in love with him," she added with conviction, even now twenty-six anniversaries later.

The wedding was wonderful, Theresa remembered. She wore a white lace gown with a full train and veil, and carried a bouquet of roses and daisies. Over 150 guests watched the happy couple say, "I do." Theresa was a bride filled with excitement, "thrilled to be taking this new step."

Having been raised a Catholic influenced Theresa's decision to wait until she was married to have intercourse, although she had dated a lot of guys and had done "everything but," as she described her pre-marital sexual experiences. Now, as a newlywed, she looked forward to this special night with her husband. "I was expecting to finally experience what a lot of my girlfriends were talking about. I was looking for bells and whistles and the earth shaking. I expected to have a lot of fun."

After the wedding reception, the couple returned to Theresa's apartment, where Bryan had already moved in his belongings. They set the mood for romance with soft music and candles. Theresa dabbed on some perfume and donned a sexy, white teddy—her "honeymoon teddy." The foreplay was enjoyable, she said. Then they tried to have intercourse.

"I felt like I was going to implode if he put his penis in me," Theresa described the sudden fear and panic that overcame her. "I felt like it was going to be awful. My body shut down. My mind was telling me, It's going to be painful. You're not big enough down there. Every time we tried to have sex my legs would clamp. I would get tense and anxious. It was like a flood of feelings. I didn't know what to do."

In many ways, the story of Theresa's unhappy wedding night is the story of vaginismus itself, a condition characterized by an extreme fear of vaginal penetration, and involuntary, uncontrollable spasms of the vaginal muscles. In the most severe cases of vaginismus, the muscles clamp so tightly that sex is virtually impossible, despite the fact that these women have healthy, normal-size vaginas. "It's like hitting a wall" is the way so many vaginismus sufferers describe their failed and all-too-frustrating attempts at intercourse. In fact, one patient reported that her husband's penis was actually red and sore after so many attempts to get past this barrier.

In Theresa's case, she and her husband continued to try to have sex, but the same thing kept happening. She was seized with anxiety and the "wall" remained as impenetrable as if it were made of bricks. The more the couple tried, the more frustrated and upset Theresa became, not knowing how to explain her reaction to Bryan, who at first seemed less concerned about the problem than his wife. "But I knew something was really wrong," Theresa said. "I felt like a failure, like some kind of freak, who couldn't do what seems to come so naturally to other women."

"Isolated" is a word Theresa used to describe her feelings as a young bride who, for some unfathomable reason, couldn't have sex with the man she loved. Who do you talk to about a problem like this? She agonized about this back then, and for many years to come. The three girlfriends she eventually told about her problem were supportive, but they didn't have a clue. Even the many professionals she went to for help over the years—primary care physicians, gynecologists, hypnotists—couldn't offer any answers. In fact, many doctors today, including both medical specialists in women's health and sex therapists, are still unfamiliar with the term vaginismus, or lack the depth of understanding necessary to treat it effectively.

Yet as isolated as Theresa felt as a woman in an unconsummated marriage, she is hardly alone. While there is no definitive study related to the incidence of vaginismus, researchers estimate that as many as 1 to 7 percent of women across cultures suffer from this condition. What's more, women tend to under-report this problem, too embarrassed to divulge their "shameful secret" even to their doctors. This shroud of silence and isolation also extends to women who suffer from painful intercourse, or dyspareunia, which is estimated to effect from 3 to 43 percent of women.[1]

* *

"Where do I start? I wanted to wait to have sex until I got married, so I did not find out about my condition until our wedding night. It was awful. I went to so many doctors I even lost count, and all of them told me I was crazy and that it was in my head. I would go to specialists, psychologists, physical therapists, etc. I did this for almost three years. In the meantime, my intimate relationship with my husband was absolutely non existent. He would not want to touch me in fear of hurting me. I felt useless as a woman; I wanted to make love to my husband but I just could not. The pain was so intense I would black out almost every time we would try. So after a couple of tries we just stopped trying."

* *

Given the prevalence and complexity of vaginismus, it's no surprise that this condition is the leading cause of unconsummated marriages around the world. In my own practice, I have seen a number of patients who, like Theresa, discovered their inability to have intercourse on their wedding night. The particulars of their stories are as individual as the women themselves, yet they all share a common thread of frustration and suffering.

One patient who came to me reported that she "cries all the time." Another feels "emotional and useless." Many grieve over the children they never had, or may never be able to conceive. Often, vaginismus sufferers believe or are told that their problem is just a case of nerves. Then days become weeks and weeks became months and years, and still they are unable to consummate their relationships.

Are you Suffering from Vaginismus?

❧ Have fear and pain stopped you from having intercourse or any form of vaginal penetration?

❧ Are you unable to use tampons, or feel like they won't fit?

❧ Are you fearful of internal gynecological examinations? Do you experience trembling, sweating, or nausea in anticipation of an examination, or at the slightest touch near your vulvar area?

❧ When you attempt intercourse, does it feel like your partner is hitting a wall?

❧ Do you avoid any kind of intimacy, even kissing, in case it might lead to your partner wanting more?

❧ Have your relationships suffered or ended because of your inability to relax with any form of penetration?

❧ When you think about sex, do you find yourself asking, Why can't I do what seems to come so naturally to other women?

If you answered "yes" to any of these questions, you may be suffering from vaginismus, a condition characterized by the extreme fear of vaginal penetration. Regardless of how long you have had vaginismus, or how hopeless you may feel at this moment, know that your vaginismus can very likely be overcome. With the proper treatment, you not only can experience intercourse, but ultimately enjoy a fulfilling sex life.

For women who live with vaginismus every day, this is a condition that extends far beyond the bedroom walls. No matter whether the situation is romantic or medical, no matter how often they tell themselves to just relax, they react to vaginal penetration with fear and pain, sometimes even nausea and fainting. It's no wonder so many women with vaginismus refer to the condition as a "nightmare."

As I've said, my own experience treating vaginismus patients dates back only to 2005, a relatively short time frame given my thirty-year career as a physician and plastic surgeon. But I can honestly say that the stories shared by my vaginismus patients—their trials as they sought help, and their triumphs after treatment—count among the most moving patient interactions I've ever had the privilege to experience.

This chapter opened with the story of Theresa, a woman who struggled with vaginismus for twenty-six years. The condition robbed her of the opportunity to bear a child and broke up her marriage for a year, but she never stopped looking for a cure.

Six months ago, Theresa contacted me. After receiving Botox treatment, Theresa and her husband subsequently achieved pain-free penetration for the first time in their marriage. "This was amazing. I was overjoyed!" Theresa's emotion could be heard in her voice. Now, several months post-Botox treatment, the couple continues to navigate their way from intercourse to the joys of sex, a process that may take persistence and continued effort after so many years in a sexless marriage.

But when it comes to vaginismus, progress can be measured in increments as well as orgasms. So, in that regard, Theresa is already a success.

References

1. Schultz, W.W., Basson R., Binik Y., Eschenbach D., Wesselmann U. and J. Van Lankveld. "Women's sexual pain and its management." *Journal of Sexual Medicine* 2 (2005): 301-16

What is Vaginismus?

Nineteenth-century American physician and surgeon James Marion Sims coined the term "vaginismus" in 1861, after observing patients such as the woman he describes in his account of an examination on page 9. Sims was not the first doctor to encounter these symptoms in female patients—written references to similar "women's diseases" go back as far as the eleventh century—but he was the first physician to both give this condition a name, and introduce the concept of widening procedures, or dilation, as a possible treatment for vaginismus after an operation.

For his significant contributions to women's health, Sims was dubbed the "father of gynecology," and his home state of South Carolina paid homage to him with a bronze monument on the statehouse grounds in Columbia. Beneath the impressive bust is a quote from Hippocrates, "Where the love of man is, there is also the love of art," and beside this an inscription that reads, "The first surgeon of the ages in ministry to women, treating alike empress and slave."

Of course, few things are as straightforward as one might wish. Sims, the respected and zealous doctor, did indeed develop techniques and instruments that advanced the study of women's reproductive health, but he also performed experimental operations on slave women to further his studies—without anesthesia, often resulting in mutilation and death.

Like the doctor who first gave this condition its name, vaginismus is also not as straightforward as some people might believe. "Oh, you're

Account of an Examination, 1861

. . . .

The most interesting point in the account of the woman was the fact that although she was married for quarter of a century, she was still a virgin. In my examination about this phenomenon, vaginal examination utterly failed... Even my very slight touch to the vaginal entrance was causing an intensive reaction. The neural system was in chaos, there was this general muscle tension. Her whole body was turning rigid intermittently and trembling. She was screaming and her eyes were glowing like mad. While tear drops were gliding down her cheeks, this situation that resembled terror and death agony was very pitiful. Despite the reflection of all of her physical pain, she was strong, staying on the examination couch, she was begging for me to go on if there was hope for her desperate condition. With all my strength, after a few minutes of thrusting, I was able to put my finger into her vagina for a few seconds, but it did not go further. There was great resistance in the vagina and a rigid contraction that lessened the sensitivity of my finger. Thus, through this examination, I realized that there was this hard-to-overcome contraction at the entrance of the vagina.

– James Marion Sims (1861)

Transactions of the Obstet. Soc. of London 3:356-7

afraid to have sex? Then just do it, for goodness sakes, and you'll be over it in no time." While far too many vaginismus sufferers have been given this kind of simplistic advice, or tell themselves something similar, this painful disorder and phobia is too complex to be overcome with these kinds of platitudes, however well meaning.

Vaginismus has both a physical and a psychological component. It varies in levels of severity, and how and when it manifests. And it has to do with sex, which we all know is the most natural thing in the world...

except when it's not. Yes, vaginismus can be successfully treated, but the first step to success is to understand what this frequently misunderstood condition really is, in order to better direct our collective energy, emotions, and efforts toward a real cure.

Involuntary Vaginal Muscle Spasms

According to the fourth version of the *Diagnostic and Statistical Manual of Mental Disorders, 4th Edition*, published in 2000 by the American Psychiatric Association, vaginismus is "a female sexual dysfunction, specifically a genital pain disorder, consisting of lifelong involuntary spasms of the vaginal muscles, not caused by a general medical condition, which interferes with intercourse causing distress and interpersonal difficulty."

The DSM–IV definition has drawn some controversy and criticism among vaginismus sufferers and clinicians alike, starting with the term "dysfunction," which implies the vagina is not acting as it should; this may not always be the case, depending on the circumstances. My own observations have confirmed that there is no debate about the reality of those "involuntary spasms."

From Sims' day through the past 150 years, this trait has been the defining diagnostic criterion for vaginismus, and I myself have witnessed the relentless grip of these muscle contractions time and time again when examining my own vaginismus patients. Even when a patient is under deep sedation—for example, a level that would allow surgery of the knee—these spasms may persist. Similar to Dr. Sims' experience described in his account of an examination, I too have barely been able to introduce my index finger into a clenched vagina, at least until the patient is given deeper levels of anesthesia.

Pinpointing the Location of the Spasm

In his early notes about vaginismus, Sims referenced the muscle contraction at the entrance of the vagina. Much more recently, the DSM–IV cites the "recurrent or persistent involuntary spasm of the musculature of the outer third of the vagina that interferes with intercourse." However,

I am not in full agreement with this latter statement because my own examinations of patients point to the entry muscle as being the culprit in most of the women who come to me suffering from vaginismus.

With the patient sedated, a necessity given her anxiety level, I begin my examination by evaluating the tightness of the lower three vaginal muscles, starting at the entry muscle of the vagina, known as the bulbocavernosum or bulbocavernosus muscle. This small muscle encircles the entry to the vagina. The same muscle is present in men and women, and is responsible for what can be thought of as a light contraction of the pelvic floor, resulting in a voluntary flicker of either the penis or clitoris. For the small size of this muscle, it is impressive how tight it can be!

● ●

"My vagina doesn't work. When it comes down to it, that's what vaginismus is."

● ●

The bulbocavernosum is the one most often in a state of spasm in women with vaginismus, contracting even during deeper levels of anesthesia. The stubborn contraction of this entry muscle is what makes many women describe their failed attempts at intercourse as "like hitting a brick wall."

During anesthesia the degree of spasm is assigned a number from one to four, with four being the most severe. The entry muscle is usually a 4+/4 meaning that maximum spasms are occurring during the initial examination.

Above the entry muscle is the pubococcygeus muscle, the "PC muscle" used in performing "Kegels" or pelvic floor muscle exercises. This is a much larger muscle than the bulbocavernosum, the entry muscle; its activation causes a strong contraction of the pelvic floor. Many researchers have implicated the PC muscle as the source of spasm in vaginismus, but in almost all of my patients I have seen only a limited amount of spasm due to contractions of this muscle. The PC muscle usually is recorded as a 0-1+/4.

A bit higher in the vagina, about midway, is the puborectalis muscle, usually the last physical barrier when it comes to achieving full intercourse. With a smaller number of my patients have I found this muscle registering a higher level of spasm, such as a 2-3+/4. What's

Two Types of Vaginismus

You may have **primary vaginismus** if you have never been able to experience any kind of vaginal penetration, though a few patients with primary vaginismus can insert a thin tampon with difficulty. In contrast, women with **secondary vaginismus** previously had a normal sex life and/or normal vaginal deliveries of children. Only later were they unable to have intercourse.

An example of a patient with secondary vaginismus is a woman who had a hysterectomy and removal of her ovaries for endometriosis when she was forty. She did well on hormone replacement therapy but discontinued this when her sister developed recurrent breast cancer. After stopping therapy, she noted excessive dryness and "tried every lube under the sun." Regardless, she started having progressively worse pain with intercourse.

At age 44, three years prior to seeing me for Botox for vaginismus, this patient stopped having intercourse all together. "I used to have a wonderful sex life, and now all we do is fight," she wrote in her pre-procedure questionnaire. "I am on the verge of a divorce." Clearly, whether the vaginismus is primary or secondary, the emotional fallout can be equally devastating.

It's important to note that, when this patient was examined under anesthesia, she had the same spasm of the entry muscle that is frequently observed in primary vaginismus patients. It seems that there is a protective reflex that causes spasm of the vaginal muscles when a woman fears the pain of penetration. Though there may be many causes of secondary vaginismus, when the condition manifests in spasm of the muscles, treatment of these secondary cases is similar to that of primary vaginismus, in that it needs to address both the physical and emotional components of the condition.

more, in some cases this is the only muscle to spasm when I perform my initial examination, which explains why some patients are able to achieve only partial intercourse.

Joan falls into this last category. She always felt that she was having normal intercourse. One day her partner, Bert, asked why she prevented him from "going in all the way?"

"I don't," Joan responded, confused by his reaction. "It feels normal to me."

The couple's inability to achieve full intercourse made me wonder whether Joan's spasms were being caused by the middle vaginal muscle. This diagnosis was confirmed when Joan's puborectalis muscle was noted to be clenched even when she was under anesthesia.

Depending on the location and degree of the muscle spasm, vaginismus can range from mild pain during intercourse, which doctors refer to as dyspareunia or painful intercourse, to a more severe burning, searing pain, to the complete inability to have any penetration, whether in the form of a penis, a speculum, a dilator, or even a self-administered small tampon.

A Phobic, Anxious Reaction

In addition to its physical attributes, vaginismus can also be character-ized in part as an exaggerated, irrational fear of penetration—a type of phobia. Like any anxiety disorder it can vary in severity. And left untreated, it can compromise your activities, your relationships, and your peace of mind.

To give you a sense of how the emotional component of vaginismus translates to everyday life, consider the following remarks from a few patients. One woman explained that when she tried to insert a tampon as a teenager, she felt "lightheaded" at the thought of it. Another patient shared a similar experience: "I never tried because the thought of it made me sick to my stomach." Yet another patient tearfully volunteered, "On my wedding night I was terrified and cried when we tried to have intercourse. It felt like a sharp, burning pain when my husband tried to penetrate me."

And then there is this patient account, which echoes the sentiments expressed in so many other stories of vaginismus: "Whenever my

The Elusive "Cure"

Women with vaginismus often try one or several of the following treatments, hoping for relief. Some of these approaches are effective in addressing milder cases of vaginismus. Others add up to weeks or even years of frustration or even destructive behavior.

Kegel exercises
Hypnotherapy
Physical therapy with or without biofeedback
Psychotherapy
Psychoanalysis
Emotional Freedom Technique (EFT)
Lubricants
Topical anesthetics
Muscle relaxants
Anti-anxiety meds
Anti-depressants
Surgical hymenectomy
Surgical vestibulectomy
Sedatives
Excess alcohol use
Hallucinogenic drugs

husband has tried insertion, I snap off just at the point of contact. It exhausts me mentally and I completely withdraw, either by crying or screaming."

Some researchers and therapists believe that the seed of vaginismus lies in psychological or emotional issues associated with penetration, and that any recurring vaginal spasms are the result of the phobia.

My clinical experience also suggests that there is some correlation between vaginismus and the psychosexual concerns reported by patients. Some of these concerns seem to have derived from a strict upbringing that strongly discouraged sexual involvement before marriage, or conveyed the message that sex is "dirty" and "boys only want one thing." In a woman susceptible to vaginismus, these messages may become even more entrenched if a sister or close relative has a child out of wedlock, resulting in increased family tension.

In addition, certain religious beliefs may help foster the development of vaginismus. Some of my patients have been taught that God punishes women who have inappropriate sexual relations. Others have had misguided graphic discussions among girlfriends about vaginas ripping and bleeding after first-time intercourse. Often women with vaginismus come to believe that their vagina is too small for a penis or any form of penetration, including a slim tampon.

While these stories strongly indicate a relationship between a patient's psychosexual concerns and vaginismus, other patient histories seem to suggest that this may not always be the case. In fact, some doctors and patients believe that vaginismus is simply a physical condition, something certain women are just born with. This camp equates vaginal spasms to, say, a facial tic, and speculate that the phobic reaction is likely a consequence of dealing with this unwanted and involuntary physical condition.

My own data suggest that family history may be positive for vaginismus, especially on the maternal side. Several patients have noted that their mothers or grandmothers also had considerable pain with first-time intercourse.

Regardless, there is no denying that every woman with vaginismus ultimately demonstrates a strong, anxious reaction in response to her vagina or vulva being touched in certain or all circumstances. For this reason, vaginismus is often labeled a "phobia," but whether this label serves is questionable. The last thing many women with vaginismus want is one more label.

Given the pain associated with intercourse, it behooves us to ask whether the involuntary muscle spasm associated with vaginismus is a phobic reaction…or simply a natural, protective response, similar to how one's hand automatically withdraws when in contact with a hot stove? However one answers that question, the fact remains: the psychological component of vaginismus, in combination with the physical reality of the involuntary muscle spasms, is what makes this condition so challenging for women to overcome.

A Search for Answers

One of my patients on the West Coast had been struggling with the symptoms of vaginismus for over a decade. She spent years going to doctors and undergoing therapy to try to overcome the condition. Yet in all of those healthcare appointments, a diagnosis of vaginismus was never mentioned. In fact, it wasn't until she did her own research on the Internet last year that she came across the term "vaginismus," and a possible treatment for the disorder using Botox.

She wrote to me, "Before I made the trip to see you in New Hampshire, I tried one last time to get treatment near home. I contacted fourteen teaching hospitals and institutions in California and Washington, with no luck. I got a lot of 'What is vaginismus?' No one could help me."

Similar stories are relayed by patients throughout the United States, in Europe, and other parts of the world. A woman in England who belongs to an online vaginismus support group shared this comment, which says it all: "I feel very vulnerable and frustrated when discussing vaginismus with a professional who hasn't got a clue what I'm experiencing or talking about."

On average, my vaginismus patients, especially women with the more severe forms of the condition, have spent between four and seven years looking for a diagnosis. They are frequently directed to therapies and treatments that may have many benefits, but fail to address the source of their inability to have intercourse. Similar to the patient from the West Coast, many women with this problem do not learn about vaginismus from their doctors, but instead on the Internet after searching terms such as "painful intercourse" or "vagina muscle tightness." I am an advocate of patients doing independent research when it comes to their health, but this is hardly a perfect solution, given the amount of misinformation that can also be found on the Internet.

It has become apparent that the medical community and patients with vaginismus need to work together to further awareness and knowledge about this condition.

V IS FOR VAGINISMUS...
AND OTHER PAINFUL DISORDERS

While the focus of this book is on vaginismus and its treatment, it's useful to have an understanding of other pain disorders involving the genitalia, especially because vaginismus is often associated with these much more commonly diagnosed conditions. In addition, and more troublesome, is that fact that vaginismus is often overlooked or treated incorrectly because it is not seen as its own medical condition.

If you have painful intercourse, or cannot have intercourse at all, my hope is that the following descriptions will help you and your healthcare providers identify the location and source of your pain to achieve the most accurate diagnosis and best course of treatment.

Vulvodynia

This condition literally means pain in the region of the vulva (dynia from the Greek word "odyne" meaning pain). The term was coined by Dr. T.G. Thomas in 1880. In a landmark study by doctors Bernard Harlow and Elizabeth Stewart,[1] it was estimated that as many as 14 million women in the United States will experience chronic vulvar pain during their lifetime.

The vulva is the outer part of the vagina consisting of the labia (labia majora and labia minora), the clitoris and clitoral hood (skin over the clitoris), and the vestibule (area just outside the entrance to the vagina, and inside and above the labia minora). Vulvodynia may present as pain in one or multiple areas of the vulva.

Vulvodynia is further defined as vulvar discomfort present for three months or more; most often described as burning pain, occurring in the absence of treatable conditions such as infections, dermatologic disorders, cancer, and neurologic disorders. It is further classified into generalized and localized pain, and may be provoked through a Q-Tip test (described later in this chapter), unprovoked, or both.

With vulvodynia the pain is often brought on by underwear or clothing rubbing against the vulva, and can at times be intensified during sexual activity. It may be related to painful intercourse (dyspareunia) or to vaginal spasm (vaginismus).

Vestibulodynia

This is a specific type of vulvodynia, where the pain is localized to the vestibule, the area just outside the entrance to the vagina, and above the inner labia. This condition was formerly known as vulvar vestibulitis syndrome (VVS), vestibular adenitis, and vulvovaginitis. (Note: Any medical term ending in "itis" refers to inflammation, yet often there is no inflammatory component, hence the newer term, vestibulodynia, is used to describe pain localized to the vestibule.)

Primary vestibulodynia means the condition has been present since the first tampon use or attempt at intercourse. Secondary vestibulodynia is diagnosed if the patient previously had no pain with tampon use and intercourse, but later develops the condition. Approximately 15 percent of women are estimated to have vestibulodynia, with a higher incidence among Hispanic women.

Associated problems:

Vulvodynia and vaginismus are sometimes associated with chronic fatigue, low back pain, migraines, and the following multiple complex pain disorders:

Interstitial cystitis (painful bladder syndrome). A chronic, painful condition of the bladder wall characterized by urinary urgency and frequency, pelvic pain, and painful intercourse.

Irritable bowel syndrome. Characterized by abdominal cramping or pain associated with a change in bowel habits, such as recurrent constipation and/or diarrhea.

Endometriosis. A condition in which the tissue that lines the inside of the uterus, called the endometrium or endometrial lining, is found growing in other areas outside of the uterus, commonly the ovaries, fallopian tubes, and nearby structures of the pelvis. This condition often causes severe pain within the lower abdomen and pelvis that may be associated with your periods each month.

Fibromyalgia. A chronic pain disorder characterized by widespread musculoskeletal aches, pain and stiffness, soft tissue tenderness, general fatigue, and sleep disturbances.

Temporomandibular joint disorder (TMJ). Acute or chronic inflammation of the temporomandibular joint, which connects the mandible, or lower jaw, to the skull.

Burning mouth syndrome. Characterized by unremitting oral burning or similar pain in the absence of detectable changes in the lining of the mouth.

Causes of Vulvodynia

While the causes of vulvodynia are elusive and virtually unknown, a great deal of research indicates that certain congenital, genetic, hormonal, and immunologic factors, as well as increased pain sensory receptors may contribute to the problem.

For example, vulvovaginal specialist Andrew T. Goldstein, MD, notes that "users of oral contraceptive pills are 660 percent more likely to develop vestibulodynia as compared to non-users."[2] In addition, a researcher at the University of Minnesota, Ruby Nguyen, PhD, has cited a nearly ten-fold increase in the risk of vulvodynia in women who have a combination of yeast infections, a history of urinary tract infections, and sexually transmitted infections.

At Cornell University, Drs. William J. Ledger and Steven S. Witkin are studying the etiology of provoked vestibulodynia to determine the events that initially trigger symptoms. They note the role of chronic inflammation as it relates to the immune system and genetic variations in combating the inflammation.

Researchers are also looking into the possible role of other factors including: inflammatory "mediators," molecules that are released by immune cells during times when harmful agents invade our body; urinary oxalates, organic acid found in urine; and nerve entrapment, repeated and long-term nerve compression, which have been implicated in some cases. In addition, increased pelvic floor muscle tone appears to be highly associated with vestibulodynia. Dr. Goldstein has recommended that patients who have vestibulodynia should be further categorized according to the likely cause of their symptoms, determined during their medical workup, to help facilitate more specific treatment.

Psychological and sexual dysfunctions do not appear to cause vulvodynia. That said, any condition involving chronic pain can have a disabling psychological impact. For women with vulvodynia, and their partners, desire is frequently compromised or completely diminished, and many sufferers become fearful of any activity that might provoke pain. Over time, its unpredictable flare-ups and recurring pain may cause patients to experience agitation, sleep disturbance, fatigue, anxiety, feelings of hopelessness, and depression.

Treatment of Vulvodynia

Different approaches may be used to address the chronic pain and other symptoms of vulvodynia. In addition, women can take measures on their own to help prevent flare-ups or further irritation. Here is a list of treatment options and tips for reducing pain.

> **Drugs.** Chronic pain specialists may recommend the use of antidepressants such as amitriptyline and nortriptyline. In lower doses, these drugs are used to help combat pain rather than for their antidepressant effects. Another drug, Gabapentin, or its generic version, Neurontin, was originally developed for the treatment of epilepsy, but has been used "off label" (meaning it is awaiting FDA approval for this specific use) to treat chronic pain conditions such as vulvodynia.

Physical therapy and biofeedback. With manual therapy of the muscles in the pelvis, stretching of soft tissue connections, and releases of trigger points (hyperirritable spots in the muscles), patients may experience diminished pelvic floor tension and increased pelvic floor strength, which could reduce vulvar pain and improve comfort with intercourse.

Botox. A Korean study reported the value of Botox used to eliminate pain in the vulva in seven patients.[3] Five of these patients required a second, larger dose, and all patients remained free of pain at their two-year follow-up. Separate research by James Presthus, MD, and Dennis Dykstra, MD, of the University of Minnesota, reports that Botox is useful not only to relieve muscular over-activity, but also has a direct action on reducing vulvar pain.[4] My own study, published in the December 2009 issue of *Plastic and Reconstructive Surgery* showed a success rate of more than 90 percent with my first twenty patients, most with the severe form of vaginismus.[5] Associated vulvodynia or vestibulodynia seems to disappear after the vaginismus is successfully treated. (See chapter 8 of this book for a detailed account of the use of Botox in treating vaginismus.)

Surgery. For what is referred to as severe "refractory" vestibulodynia, meaning not yielding readily to treatment, patients may be offered the option of a vestibulectomy. This is considered because a suspected cause of vulvodynia is that too many nerve endings in parts of the vulva are causing the pain. With a vestibulectomy, a portion of the vestibule is removed with surgery and the remaining cuff of vagina is advanced to close the defect. Dr. Presthus, of the Botox study noted above, has had personal experience with vestibulectomy, and feels that Botox offers a less invasive option for severe cases of vestibulodynia.

Tips for Alleviating the Pain of Vulvodynia

- Wear 100 percent cotton underwear, though not while sleeping.
- Avoid douching, washcloths, and panty liners. Gently wash with mild soaps.

- Rinse after urination and pat the area dry. Plain petroleum jelly (Vaseline) can be used if the skin is dry.

- During menstruation, use unscented, non-dyed cotton pads.

- Use lubricants during intercourse. Some women with vulvodynia favor natural oils such as olive or sesame seed oils.

- Topical anesthetics such as 2 percent Xylocaine jelly or 5 percent Xylocaine ointment can help numb the painful areas during intercourse, but all topical anesthetics cause some burning on initial application. Topical estrogens or a combination of estradiol 0.03 percent and testosterone 0.1 percent may be effective.

- Cool gel packs or other mild cold applications can be soothing, but don't overuse.

Getting to the Root of the Pain

"It hurts when I try to have intercourse."

"It hurts down there."

"Sex is impossible. Every time we try, it's like hitting a wall."

When a woman comes into a doctor's office with these symptoms, how is the source of the pain determined? It is often assumed that painful intercourse resides in the area of the vulva, which would suggest a diagnosis of vulvodynia, or maybe vestibulodynia. But what is the patient really feeling when she says "it hurts"?

Like so many cases that involve chronic pain, it can be difficult for someone with pain in the area of her genitalia to describe or even know exactly where it hurts. And to complicate matters further, when a woman retreats from contact or penetration, is she reacting from pain, or from the fear associated with pain?

Jennifer, a 22-year-old patient, speaks to the challenge, and importance, of getting to the root of the pain. Jennifer struggled for three years with her inability to have sex with her boyfriend. "My partner and I have tried penetration a lot and have not gotten very far at all," she shared. "It feels like I'm being split almost. It's extremely painful."

Jennifer was accompanied during her appointment by her mother, a nurse. We could feel Jennifer's distress as she spoke about how her condition had complicated her relationships past and present.

"I feel inferior, almost not like a woman because I can't be intimate with my boyfriend and share this experience with him. I do love him," she explained tearfully. "I want that part of our relationship, but this is on the verge of ruining it." Jennifer also shared that she had tried to address the problem by working with dilators to stretch her vagina for about seven months at her ob-gyn's office, but she hadn't progressed very far.

The Q-Tip Test

As I do with all my patients, I followed up my conversation with Jennifer and her mother with an examination called the Q-Tip Test, to determine whether there was any pain involving her external genital organs. In this test, gentle pressure is applied with a cotton-tipped applicator on the patient's inner thighs, the mons pubis, and around the entrance to the vagina. For women without vulvar pain, the Q-Tip test is painless. In contrast, for women with vulvodynia, this gentle test can result in varying levels of pain from mild to excruciating, and the pain may be localized to one or more areas. When the touch of the Q-Tip elicits pain specifically in the vestibule, for example, this suggests provoked vestibulodynia.

"No pain," Jennifer reports when the swab runs along her inner thigh. She gives the same answer when the Q-Tip touches her mons pubis, as well as her left labium majorum. Then the Q-Tip lightly touches her right labia majorum and she jolts and pulls away. From her strong reaction, one might assume a diagnosis of vulvodynia. But obtaining the correct diagnosis also means asking the correct questions.

"Where is the pain?" she is asked.

Surprisingly, instead of indicating her right labia, the area which elicited a response when touched, Jennifer reports that the pain is inside her vagina. In medical school we are taught, "Listen to the patient. She can tell you the diagnosis." It appears Jennifer's response is indeed telling a very different story.

The stroke of the Q-Tip resulted in a major visceral reaction, but not because a painful part of the vulva had been stimulated. For lack of a better term, this could be called "pseudo-vulvodynia." The fact that Jennifer has "referred" pain inside her vagina may indicate a diagnosis of vaginismus, spasms within the vagina, rather than true vulvodynia. Similarly, her inability to have pain-free intercourse may stem from vaginal spasm rather than vulvodynia.

Other patients have the same reaction, particularly those with severe vaginismus who report similar referred pain, and react to the touch of a Q-Tip with sweating, nausea, or withdrawal. Some patients do not permit an examination in this area while they are awake.

Given how frequently vaginismus is misdiagnosed, physicians and therapists dealing with these pain disorders should always ask during the Q-Tip test: Where is the pain? With this information, and a better understanding of the distinctions between vulvodynia and vaginismus, we can help assure that patients like Jennifer and countless others receive the proper diagnosis and treatment.

References:

1. Harlow, B.L. and E.G. Stewart. "A population-based assessment of chronic unexplained vulvar pain: have we underestimated the prevalence of vulvodynia?" *Journal of the American Medical Women's Association* 58 (2003): 82-88.
2. Goldstein, Andrew T., MD. Editorial, *Journal of Sex Medicine* 6 (2009): 3227-3229.
3. Yoon, H. et al. "Botulinum Toxin A for the Management of Vulvodynia." *International Journal of Impotence Research* 19 (2007): 84-87.
4. Presthus, J.B. and D.D. Dykstra. "Botulinum Toxin Therapy for Vulvodynia." *National Vulvodynia Association News* 12, no. 3 (2007): 1-5.
5. Pacik, P.T. "Viewpoint: Botox Treatment for Vaginismus." *Plastic & Reconstructive Surgery* 24 (2009): 455e-456e.

GETTING THE RIGHT DIAGNOSIS

The voice on the other end of the phone belonged to a vulvovaginal specialist who treats hundreds of patients a year. One of her patients had recently contacted me about treating her vaginal spasms with Botox, hence my phone call to this respected doctor to discuss the case.

"Vaginismus is a word that should be removed from the scientific lexicon," the doctor flatly stated. "The term is outdated," she insisted. "Vaginismus doesn't exist."

The conversation, short and direct, gave me pause. At first, I was intimidated, comparing in my mind this seasoned doctor's experience to my more limited history treating women with vaginismus. Most of us know how easy it is to be swayed by medical specialists, and often with good reason. After all, we rely on experts for their expertise.

But what about my own observations and treatment outcomes? What about the vaginal muscle spasms that I had witnessed while examining patients in my surgical center? Over the past five years, I had successfully treated approximately one hundred women with severe vaginismus through a program involving a combination of vaginal Botox injections, progressive dilation, counseling, and follow-up support. Many medical providers have dedicated a large portion of their careers to treating vaginismus using other treatment methods, and they too have had successful results.

Nonetheless, for a significant portion of women, their vaginismus remains undiagnosed or misdiagnosed for years. By the time patients come to me, many of them had long histories of failed efforts to overcome their condition, yet they were able to achieve intercourse within weeks or a few months after my program of treatment.

Vaginismus doesn't exist? Tell that to all the women who have been diagnosed incorrectly and undergone vestibulectomies—removing the cuff of the vagina to reduce the number of nerve endings—yet still feel pain and an aversion to penetration. Vaginismus doesn't exist? Tell that to the patients who have undergone hymenectomies, sometimes more than once, to remove the membrane that covers the vaginal opening—yet still they can't experience intercourse. Not only do these types of surgeries periodically fail to treat vaginismus, but they can also lead to scarring, which in and of itself can cause pain.

"My doctor scheduled me for a hymenectomy because he was concerned I was anxious over the pain of it [the hymen] tearing," shared one patient. "I went in for surgery to remove my hymen. It took about six weeks for the area to heal. I was told that once it did heal, I would have to use vaginal dilators to help loosen the PC muscles and prep my vagina for sex. But when the time came for me to use the dilators, I tried once and it hurt so bad that I never did it again. Once again, I went into panic mode and could not even look at my vagina in the mirror without feeling queasy."

Why must so many patients, including the woman just quoted, have to go through this kind of hardship when seeking a cure? Why is vaginismus so often overlooked?

One problem is that, for whatever reason, there is a dearth of medical literature about vulvar disorders in general, and vaginismus in particular. The American College of Obstetricians and Gynecologists, for example, provides no guidelines regarding the manner in which vaginal spasms in vaginismus should be identified and measured, nor does an official gynecological diagnostic system exist for vaginismus.[1] This is just one reason why many doctors and therapists, including those specializing in women's health, have never even heard of vaginismus, or fail to diagnose it.

In addition, many research papers on vulvar disorders fail to distinguish between vaginismus and vulvodynia. Instead, the conditions are simply referenced together. My conversations with other doctors and therapists also confirm this lack of distinction. A woman who reports pain with intercourse is much more likely to be diagnosed with vulvodynia, or sometimes more specifically with provoked vestibulodynia. Further, if vaginismus is diagnosed along with vulvodynia, it is typically relegated as a secondary problem.

During my conversation with the vulvovaginal specialist about our mutual patient, I realized that part of the issue was that the physician was a specialist, which "confers a false sense of certainty," as the author Jerome Groopman, MD, wrote in his book *How Doctors Think*. Specialists are susceptible to what is called diagnosis momentum, meaning that once an authoritative physician has fixed a label to the problem it usually stays firmly attached, because the specialist is usually right. This is related to a phenomenon called "confirmation bias," which means paying attention to data that support the presumed diagnosis, and minimizing data that contradict it.

In hindsight, it is no wonder that I received such a brusque response from this specialist. I was challenging the manner in which vulvovaginal patients are most often diagnosed and treated. The specialist was reluctant to conclude that vulvodynia, the "label" that has stayed firmly attached by the medical community, was not the primary diagnosis for our patient. But, in fact, almost all of our patients who cannot have intercourse do NOT have pain in the vulvar area. They have pain only when penetration is attempted, whether through the use of a tampon, finger, speculum, dilator or penis. All this strongly indicates a diagnosis of vaginismus.

Seeing is Believing

My own experiences treating women with vaginismus have caused me to view this condition in a manner that, admittedly, may run contrary to conventional wisdom. It is my opinion that vulvodynia and vaginismus are distinct medical conditions. Both involve pain disorders in the area of the genitalia, but the root of the pain stems from very different sources. With respect to vaginismus, the pain and associated fear appear to be directly related to the vaginal spasms. In comparison, with vulvodynia, the sensitivity is related to the vulva itself.

During discussions with colleagues and patients, it has become apparent that vulvodynia is the "default" diagnosis among medical specialists, and that there is not enough focus on vaginismus as the primary diagnosis. We need to change the manner in which these conditions are diagnosed. It is necessary to diagnose vaginismus as the primary condition in those patients who are unable to have intercourse because of the fear of pain, and we must treat the condition accordingly.

The opinions in this book are also based on vaginal examinations conducted while vaginismus patients are heavily sedated or under anesthesia. These examinations provide an opportunity to study and observe the root source of the pain, which provides insights relatively few physicians or therapists are able to achieve. For example, many sex counselors are not licensed to perform physical examinations. Gynecologists can provide physical examinations, but without anesthesia they are rarely able to do so. In fact, most women with severe vaginismus are likely to jump off the table! Even physical therapists specializing in pelvic floor conditions are at a disadvantage because, without the benefit of sedation, any insertion of the finger or manipulation is likely to be difficult or even impossible to achieve with severe vaginismus.

In short, most patients presenting with pain in the area of the vulva have not been examined under anesthesia. And, without the benefit of sedation, it is almost impossible to determine the source of the pain, such as the presence and severity of vaginal spasm. As a result, many cases of vaginismus have been improperly diagnosed.

In the operating room, specialists can directly witness the spasms that result from vaginismus. For that matter, so have the patients' husbands or partners, who often accompany me when I perform an examination. In almost every patient, the entry muscle is clamped and shut tight like a fist. There is barely a pinhole opening. Occasionally, other muscles of the vagina are also affected. Most telling is that the spasms persist, even under deep levels of anesthesia. The severity of their grip results in a very real physical barrier to penetration.

Seeing these spasms in case after case explains many of the descriptions provided by vaginismus patients to their doctors and therapists. It explains the sensation of "hitting a wall" during intercourse. It also clarifies the aversion to any form of penetration, whether with a tampon, finger, speculum, dilator, or penis. And with each attempt at penetration, the pain or fear of pain is reinforced or intensified. The inability to achieve vaginal penetration is not because of pain in the vulva, but rather because of the severe spasm of the entry muscle.

This only reinforces my belief that vaginismus must be considered a separate medical condition from vulvodynia, even if the two disorders are associated. By opening our eyes to the possibility that vaginismus (muscle spasm), not vulvodynia (pain in the region of the vulva), is the primary diagnosis, the medical community can do a much better job in helping women avoid needless procedures, while alleviating their suffering much more effectively.

Lilly and Don

By the time Lilly and Don made the seventeen-hour drive to see me for treatment, they had been in a virtually sexless marriage for four years. According to some reports, about 25 percent of all marriages are "sexless," meaning that the couple has sex fewer than one to two dozen times a year. Other sources define a sexless marriage as one in which the couple has sex no more than five to ten times a year. "I had only been able to receive penetration one or two times," Lilly had explained in her pre-procedure questionnaire. "It wasn't painful, but uncomfortable, like friction and burning. We thought maybe it was nerves or something but it only got worse."

Prior to coming to me, Lilly, 23, had been diagnosed with provoked vestibulodynia, when the touch of the Q-Tip elicits pain specifically in the vestibule or outer entrance to the vagina. To overcome the problem, Lilly and Don had already tried one year of counseling. Lilly also had been taking anti-anxiety drugs for one year, and had participated in six months of physical therapy. Nothing seemed to be working.

In many ways, Lilly's experience mirrors that of many vaginismus patients. In addition to her inability to have intercourse, she also couldn't tolerate gynecological examinations. "My legs would shake and I would panic and try to pull away," she reported, "even though I didn't want to." She had never been able to insert tampons. And while she wanted to be intimate with her husband, her pain and fear far outweighed her desire. In their more recent years of attempted love-making, she had given Don strict instructions not to touch her below the waist. At this point, the hardship of this condition was taking a toll on both these young people and their relationship.

As is the case with so many patients, the unique personalities of Lilly and her husband became known and appreciated during the course of treatment. Lilly had a winning smile and big, blue eyes. Her husband, Don, was a mathematician. In fact, after the procedure, Don did the best job of any spouse in terms of tracking his wife's dilation schedule, right down to the second! Through conversations, it soon became clear that this was a couple that didn't like to keep regular hours. When called at their hotel around nine the evening before Lilly's procedure, Don asked where they could get breakfast later that night!

The next morning when Lilly and Don arrived for their procedure, it was clear that Lilly was scared and Don was quite anxious. As always, one of the first procedures performed after a patient arrives is an external physical examination to determine the source of the pain. This starts with the Q-Tip test discussed in the previous chapter.

When Lilly was tested with a Q-Tip along her inner thighs and mons pubis she was fine. But as the applicator advanced toward her vulva, Lilly began closing her thighs and retreating on the table, as much as she tried to stay under control. Higher pain scores were recorded when examining her labia, and the attempt to examine the vestibule met with a strong response: she nearly jumped off the table. Lilly was asked to differentiate between her fear and pain but she could not.

It's understandable how, at this point, Lilly might have received a diagnosis of provoked vestibulodynia as the primary problem. And, given this conclusion, some physicians would have likely recommended surgery to address the pain. Many women have lived this exact scenario, yet after all was cut and done, they saw little or no improvement in their condition. But Lilly's story continues.

During the early light anesthesia induction, more information about the source of her pain came to light. Once Lilly was able to relax thanks to sedation, it was possible to achieve an external examination without her withdrawing. During the examination, a lack of hygiene in the vulvar area was observed, undoubtedly the cause of her reported recurrent yeast infections. It became apparent that Lilly, otherwise meticulous in her appearance, wasn't even comfortable touching herself enough to wash properly. There was no reaction when Lilly's outer vulva was examined. As the examination advanced to the vestibule to determine the level of spasm of the entry muscle, however, Lilly began withdrawing again and further examination was impossible.

At this point Lilly was asleep and would remember nothing. Her husband, on the other hand, would probably remember everything. He stood at the foot of the table, looking a bit pale, and witnessed the vaginal spasms that had been preventing his wife from having intercourse. Even after a large dose of anesthetic, Lilly's vaginal entry muscle, the bulbocavernosum, was still in a profound state of spasm. Here, yet again, was the "wall," a clear indicator not of vulvodynia or vestibulodynia but of severe vaginismus.

Flash forward to an uplifting end to this story: Lilly's Botox procedure went smoothly, and immediately afterwards, she was able to use the largest dilator in the recovery room. Lilly continued to dilate after she returned home, and two weeks later she wrote to me that she and Don had achieved tip-only intercourse. Over the next months, Lilly also has benefitted from continued physical therapy, and both she and Don have been working with sex therapists together and individually to strengthen their relationship in bed and beyond.

References:

1. Reissing, E.E. et al., "Does vaginismus exist? A critical review of the literature." *The Journal of Nervous and Mental Disease* 187, no. 5 (1999): 261-271; and "Vaginal spasm, pain and behaviour: an empirical investigation of the diagnosis of vaginismus." *Archives of Sexual Behaviour* 33, no. 1 (2004): 5-17.

WHY ME?
THE CAUSES OF VAGINISMUS

"As I was growing up I often heard stories about first-time intercourse, how painful it is, the bleeding, my hymen breaking. I never thought it would affect me so badly."

So began Zahara's account of her long and emotional journey to search for a cure for vaginismus. Zahara is a former patient who travelled from England for treatment. A practicing Muslim, she and her husband met at university when they were both nineteen years old. They agreed to wait until they were married to have intercourse.

When the big day arrived seven years later, Zahara described her wedding as "the perfect fairy tale …the most wonderful day of my life." The couple wanted to have a baby right away, so what better time to try and conceive than on their honeymoon?

"On the wedding night we tried intercourse and didn't think much of it when it didn't happen," Zahara said. "I thought, It will happen in the next few days. The whole world does it. How hard can it be? But on our honeymoon we were surprised and disappointed to find that we just could not seem to consummate our relationship."

For Zahara and her husband, days of failed attempts at intercourse became weeks, then months. She pursued counseling, had a hymenectomy, and consulted with several gynecologists. But nothing changed.

As the couple approached their second anniversary, Zahara's condition began to affect her emotionally and physically. "I became terrified of the pain I was convinced I would feel," she articulated. "Every time we tried it felt like there was no room for anything to go in. It felt blocked.

"I visited my nurse after four or five months," Zahara continued. "She told me that I just needed to try harder and to relax. We had tried countless times, yet any attempt caused so much pain and discomfort. I went back to the nurse a few more times only to hear the same things. She even tried to do a Pap smear test on me twice. It was not happening and I knew something was seriously wrong. Sex had become the 'impossible' now."

When will it happen? Will it ever happen? Zahara recalled wondering during those difficult months. She elaborated, "These questions ran through my mind every day. Relatives and friends were constantly asking me, 'When are you having babies?' I was feeling pressure now. It was on my mind constantly. I was so lost. I would stare at couples and think, They must be normal. Why is this happening to us? It started taking over my life."

Zahara's experience begs the following question: What caused her vaginismus? After all, she was a healthy, young woman in a loving relationship. She was eager to consummate her marriage and start a family. Why was she unable to have sex? Did she suddenly develop a case of nerves on her wedding night? Did some emotional event in her past trigger this phobia and begin the cycle of fear and spasms? Did her subsequent attempts at intercourse and the fear of pain contribute to, or reinforce, the vaginal spasms? Was it simply genetics? Was Zahara predisposed to a physical condition in which her pelvic floor muscles spasmed involuntarily, the same way some people might present with facial tics or other physiological responses, irrelevant of emotional triggers? Why Zahara? Why you? Why anyone?

The unsettling answer to those questions is simply this: Nobody knows for sure. When it comes to either vaginismus or to phobias in general, much remains a mystery. Some studies, for example, suggest that phobias may run in families. Genetics may play a role, or you may have "learned" a phobia by observing or hearing about a family member's reaction to a situation.

Zahara's story seems to support this last notion. "Leading up to my wedding I kept hearing the silly old wives' tales about how first-time sex

Getting to the Root of the Problem...

Below, women with vaginismus share their feelings about what might have caused their condition.

In January of 2004, I went in to see my doctor and be put on birth control. I was getting married in May and I wanted the pill to be 100 percent effective by the night of my wedding. I was told after I arrived at the office that a pelvic exam would have to be performed to check for certain things before they could give me a prescription. I was very nervous and upset, but I figured that this was something that I had to do. I had to be a woman. When the doctor attempted to insert the speculum, I freaked out. I began to shake and shiver and break out in hives. I began sweating profusely and crying uncontrollably. It was like I was having a seizure. No matter how much I tried to relax and calm down, my body would not respond. I had not told anyone about being abused as a child, but it never crossed my mind that maybe this was the reason that I was panicking.

Four years ago, I experienced extreme pain during a routine Pap smear, and can remember from that point onwards sex became difficult and eventually impossible.

I just think I am scared because I grew up in a strict household where my parents always kept track of us. We always had to lie to get out of the house. We were never allowed to date or talk to boys.

I was not aware that I had a problem until my honeymoon night. However, looking back, I was never able to insert a tampon. My mum always used to tell me that it could get lost or cause toxic shock syndrome. I suppose that has always stuck in my head. I was extremely anxious about sex prior to being married. The only information I had about sex was negative from my mum and Gran and I was raised in a Christian family from birth so was always taught that sex before marriage was wrong.

I have no bad sexual experiences whatsoever. In fact, I have no idea where this problem stemmed from. Before attempting to have sex I had no fear whatsoever and was very confident. Apparently this is in my deep subconscious.

is so painful, how you bleed," she explained. "I was even told that you can pass out with the pain. I just tried to ignore them. I realize now what a load of rubbish it was," she said. "What I didn't realize was that I was storing all this information subconsciously."

Studies also suggest brain chemicals and traumatic experiences may influence the development of phobias. Specific to vaginismus, research has provided even more clues as to its possible origins. In 1994, for example, British researchers Jane Ogden and Elaine Ward conducted a qualitative study[1] on vaginismus that concluded that the three highest ranked characteristics of women who suffer from vaginismus are usually:

1. Fear of painful sex; fear of pain at insertion.

2. Strict religious upbringing where sex was viewed as wrong or not discussed.

3. Early childhood traumatic experiences, not necessarily sexual in nature.

More recently, research headed up by Elke Reissing looked at whether childhood sexual abuse played a role in the later development of vaginismus.[2] The authors used structured questionnaires to compare women with vaginismus to those without, using a number of matches for comparisons.

The research indicated that women with vaginismus were twice as likely to have been sexually abused as children. While this actually represents a small percentage of the population, I do have a few patients who fall within this category. This finding was in contrast to physical abuse during childhood, in which no correlation could be found to vaginismus.

My own pre-procedure questionnaires explore in detail a range of psychosexual events that shed light on possible causes of a patient's condition. These questionnaires not only elicit any history of sexual molestation, but also other psychosexual factors, such as the influence of strict religious and/or sexual upbringing, traumatic events such as a sibling who conceived out of wedlock, which can cause significant family tension, and family pressure to wait until marriage to have intercourse.

The questionnaires also have illuminated that many patients are fearful of the pain of having intercourse for the first time. They believe their vagina is too small and will rip and bleed during sex. One patient described excruciating pain when her boyfriend suddenly entered her without preparation. Other women have cited the fear of gynecological examinations, giving birth, and other issues. For example, a patient reported that she was terrified of intercourse because an uncle died at a young age from AIDS.

With this broader brushstroke, a remarkably high number of our vaginismus patients—80 to 90 percent—report a history of psychosexual traumatic events. While I want to be careful not to jump to conclusions as I continue my data analysis, I do feel that these findings strongly counter the thinking in much of the current literature that no one knows the causes of vaginismus. What seems to be increasingly clear is that, at its root, vaginismus stems from a protective reflex of vaginal spasm in response to the fear of anticipated pain.

Returning to the Reissing study, this work also found that women who suffer from vaginismus or dyspareunia (painful intercourse) had less sexual desire, sexual arousal, sexual pleasure, and self-stimulation than women without those conditions. Further, women with vaginismus had significantly less self awareness of their own sexuality compared to women who do not have vaginismus. In my own practice, I have found that many of my patients are uninformed about sexuality, and in fact a number of these women have told me they do not know where their vagina is located.

There also appear to be various degrees of vaginismus. This contin-uum ranges from women with dyspareunia resulting in mild to moderate discomfort, to women with severe forms of the condition, in which the burning pain lasts for several days. The degree of burning appears to be related to the intensity of the vaginal spasms.

It is not surprising that researchers have found both dyspareunia and vaginismus are under-diagnosed. In a publication from Milan, Italy, entitled "Etiology and Diagnosis of Coital Pain," author A. Graziottin concluded that painful intercourse may affect as many as 10 to 15 percent of sexually active fertile women, and 39 percent of postmeno-pausal women.[3] As referenced earlier, researchers suggest the incidence of vaginismus is between 1 and 7 percent, about the same percentage as men with erectile dysfunction.

Given the prevalence of dyspareunia and vaginismus, it is encour-aging to note that both of those conditions were included in the international classification on female sexual disorders published in 2008. The recognition of these conditions may now make it possible for treat-ments of dyspareunia and vaginismus to be covered by insurance.

From Cause... to Cure

When treating most medical or psychological conditions, ideally we want to address the underlying causes of the problem, not just the symptoms. Given what we do know about vaginismus, women can rest assured that this problem is not just in their minds. The spasms are real and appear to be a protective reflex to what is perceived as a potentially painful experience. Even women who previously enjoyed intercourse and only developed vaginismus later in life (secondary vaginismus) may be noted to have spasm of the vaginal muscles.

Although it may not be possible to identify what triggered the vaginismus, it is still beneficial for women to evaluate whether a certain experience prompted their fears of penetration. This soul searching may lead to a greater self awareness. The personal insights obtained may also contribute to a more global discussion about how families and society can stop the types of traumatic events and misguided messages about sexuality that put too many girls and young women at risk for this condition.

That said, while psychotherapy or sexual counseling often provides significant progress for patients with mild vaginismus, in more severe cases such therapy alone may not alleviate the physical reality of vaginal spasm. In severe cases, the treatment of vaginismus solely through counseling or other traditional therapies may even become a set-up for further disappointment. The longer it appears that it is not possible to "talk your way out of the problem," the deeper the frustration.

Clearly, vaginismus is too complex to be viewed as a straightforward medical, biological, or psychological condition. Some cases may respond to one form of treatment. Others will not. That is why it is critical to classify the level of vaginismus when weighing treatment options. (How to determine your level of vaginismus is explained in full detail in the next chapter.)

The emerging research supports a multi-faceted approach to achieve a successful outcome. My own treatment program (as described in detail in Chapter 7) combines the use of Botox injections to the affected vaginal muscles, vaginal dilation under anesthesia, and post-procedure care and counseling.

For Zahara, whose story opened this chapter, this comprehensive treatment program was the solution she was looking for. "It was day twelve we attempted intercourse for the second time," she shared. "The first time it didn't happen. I left the dilator in for a good three to four hours and we attempted penetration. It wasn't full-on intercourse but he was able to enter me without any problem. I felt a little discomfort, maybe a stretching pain for few minutes. It was beyond belief and I was speechless. Something we had waited two years for had finally happened."

Zahara had travelled from the United Kingdom to my practice in New Hampshire because she couldn't find a doctor in her country who knew anything about Botox for vaginismus. Ironically, when Zahara and her husband arrived home after their trip to the States, they finally received a long-awaited letter scheduling an appointment with a counseling service. "I binned it!" Zahara said.

References:

1. Ward E. and E. Ogden. "Experiencing vaginismus-sufferers' beliefs about causes and effects." *Journal of Sex and Marital Therapy* 9 (1994): 33-45.

2. Reissing, E.D.; Binik, Y.M.; Khalifé, S.; Cohen, D. and R. Amsel. "Etiological correlates of vaginismus: sexual and physical abuse, sexual knowledge, sexual self-schema, and relationship adjustment." *Journal of Sex and Marital Therapy* 29 (2003): 47-59.

3. Graziottin, A. "Etiology and diagnosis of coital pain." *Journal of Endocrinological Investigation* 26, no. 3 (2003): 115-21.

How Bad is Bad?
The Five Levels of Vaginismus

Amy tells her doctor, "I think I can insert a tampon, but the idea of having it in me during the day scares me."

Parminder describes her situation, "I will allow a gynecologist to touch the area, but not to insert anything."

When asked about sex, Mary reports that she doesn't experience pain when her vagina is fondled or during oral sex, "but it's been so long I'm not sure."

Deanna shares this story from her honeymoon: "Whenever we would attempt to make love I would have panic attacks, tremors, cry, and a fear would overtake me."

And Julia describes her experience working with a pelvic floor physical therapist after she was diagnosed with vaginismus: "For the first few months, she wasn't able to even touch me. I fought back. I could tell she had never dealt with a case as severe as mine. She wanted to help, but was often stuck on what to do next. My physical therapist ended the sessions because she didn't know what else she could do for me."

These are the experiences of five different women, all of whom have been diagnosed with vaginismus. For each of these patients, vaginal penetration was impossible. However, it is obvious that even while these women share the same diagnosis, they vary dramatically in their responses to gynecological examinations, sex, or vaginal penetration using a tampon or dilator.

For some women with vaginismus, the pain and anxiety threshold is high enough that maybe, just maybe, they can remain calm on the examining table so long as the doctor doesn't attempt an internal examination. For others, even the loving touch of a husband or partner catapults them into defensive mode, causing them to react with such negative emotions and physical withdrawal that even they are at a loss as to how to explain their response.

Stratifying vaginismus patients according to the severity of their condition has a huge impact on the success, or failure, of a wide variety of treatments. I have noted that patients are able to classify themselves according to the Lamont classification system and their history is consistent with my findings under anesthesia.

How strongly a woman reacts to attempts at vaginal penetration can provide her doctor or therapist with important insights, not just in terms of confirming a diagnosis of vaginismus, but in terms of determining what type of treatment is necessary to address the problem. Women who can tolerate the use of tampons, for example, may have success with some of the more conservative treatments for vaginismus such as dilators, pelvic floor physical therapy, biofeedback, and/or counseling. In contrast, for women who experience higher degrees of fear and pain, such efforts, at least on their own, may do little or nothing to alleviate the severe vaginal spasms that partially define their condition.

Given the importance of differentiating the degrees of vaginismus, the good news is that there already exists a classification system developed by a Canadian doctor, J.A. Lamont, and first published in 1978 in the *American Journal of Obstetrics and Gynecology*.[1] The Lamont classification system stratifies vaginismus into four levels of severity.

Lamont's Study: How Do You Respond to a Vaginal Examination?

In Lamont's study of eighty women with vaginismus, the shortest duration of vaginismus was one month, and the longest duration was eighteen years. The average patient suffered from vaginismus for about three years. Average age of the patients was 26-27, and the oldest patient was 58. Most of the patients were married. In Lamont's series, hymenectomy was helpful in only one patient. I have found that none of our patients benefited from hymenectomy.

Classification and Degree	Number of Patients
First degree: perineal and levator spasm – relieved with reassurance	27
Second degree: perineal spasm – maintained throughout pelvic	21
Third degree: levator spasm and elevation of buttocks	18
Fourth degree: levator and perineal spasm, elevation; adduction and retreat	10
Refused examination	4

In my own experience with patients, there is considerable accuracy when my patients use this classification system. The same withdrawal patterns that are described when undergoing a gynecological examination are also present for patients in the early stages of anesthesia at the time of the Botox treatment. Level 1 patients are able to undergo an initial examination with light sedation, whereas considerable anesthesia is needed for me to properly examine a Level 4 or 5 patient. These patients with more severe levels of vaginismus show considerable retreat during the early stages of anesthesia, and examination is not possible until deeper levels of anesthesia are achieved.

Lamont developed the classification system using a study involving eighty patients who had a history of fear of penetration and generalized tightness of the pelvic floor. Each woman was assigned a level of vaginismus based on her history of the condition, and her doctor's observations during gynecological examinations. This is of note, because the inability to use tampons and difficulty with gynecological examinations are non-sexual events; this history is also important in establishing a diagnosis of vaginismus in the patient referred for sexual aversion and her inability to have intercourse.

In the Lamont classification system, Level 1 vaginismus is described as spasm of the pelvic floor that can be relieved with reassurance. This is the lowest level of vaginismus. If you fall into this category, you can have internal examinations and penetration, but it takes teamwork and patience from both you and your doctor to enable this to happen.

In Level 2 vaginismus, generalized spasm of the pelvic floor is present as a steady state, despite reassurance. You can be told to relax, but the advice yields no results; your vaginal muscles remain constricted. The fact that vaginismus patients don't have the ability—no matter how much they may want to—to voluntarily relax their vaginal muscles has been further documented during electromyography (EMG) examinations of the pelvic floor. The EMG examination demonstrates that the heightened pelvic floor spasm of vaginismus is unable to return to a normal, less spastic baseline unless treatment is instituted.

In Level 3 vaginismus, the pelvic floor spasm is sufficiently severe that the patient elevates her buttocks in an attempt to avoid being examined. In essence, the fear makes her physically react in a way that prevents a doctor from even looking at her vagina, let alone inserting a speculum or allowing a Pap smear, for example.

In Level 4 vaginismus, the most severe form of vaginismus according to Lamont, the patient totally withdraws by elevating her buttocks, retreating, and tightly closing the thighs to prevent any examination. If this is you, your behavior speaks volumes about what is clearly a deep and abiding fear of painful vaginal penetration, and why you can't just talk your way out of it.

And then there is my patient, Kelsie, who took the Lamont classification system one level further. When Kelsie arrived for treatment she had been suffering with vaginismus for over six years. She was asked to classify her degree of vaginismus based on the Lamont system.

Kelsie read through the descriptions of Lamont's four levels of vaginismus, but felt her own symptoms were off the charts, so to speak. During attempted examinations, for example, Kelsie experienced sweating, panic attacks, lightheadedness, and nausea. She also felt like she was going to faint, and had the impulse to attack the doctor to protect herself. Because these behaviors weren't reflected in Lamont's four-tiered system, Kelsie suggested adding a Level 5, which more accurately describes her experience. Other patients have reported trembling, nausea, vomiting, a desire to run away, or going unconscious. In fact, while most of the patients seen at my practice are a Lamont Level 4, there are enough patients with these extreme reactions that I have incorporated this new level into my own vocabulary when evaluating a woman's symptoms.

How important is it to incorporate the Lamont classification system in a strategy for addressing vaginismus? Critically important. In fact, it could be equated to the importance of staging cancer, which is routinely done prior to treatment. Any doctor who treats cancer needs to know the severity of the disease. For example, a doctor would not treat a melanoma without first measuring the size of the cancer, determining the thickness of the tumor, understanding the microscopic features—what the cells look like—and whether or not there are metastases. These factors are the basis for staging, and lead to different types of treatment, which in turn are related to the outcome.

The same concept holds true for vaginismus patients, although of course there are a few distinctions. With cancer, the doctor stages the disease, according to a well accepted staging nomenclature that takes into account factors such as cellular structure, the size of the tumor, and whether it has metastasized. With vaginismus, the patient determines her own Lamont level.

I request all of my patients perform a self-evaluation because I have found that they are quite accurate in their assessment of their condition. This crucial information can make all the difference between success and failure during treatment.

Without knowing the severity of vaginismus, what often results are situations like Emily's, whose pelvic floor physical therapist gave up on her after twenty sessions. This therapist used her finger to try to manually stretch Emily's vaginal muscles, under the assumption that they were foreshortened from disuse, similar to the way you need to stretch the muscles in your arm after it's been in a cast, to re-establish range of motion.

Physical therapy and this kind of stretching does indeed serve many patients, yet in Emily's case it proved a waste of time, in fact a set-back, given the emotional toll of "failing" another therapy. And why was it a failure? Because Emily turned out to be a Lamont Level 4 patient. And for Level 4 patients, it is much more difficult, and maybe even impossible, to alleviate the involuntary vaginal spasms through manual stretching.

Emily's story exemplifies why classification of the severity of vaginismus is vital information for every healthcare professional treating this condition. Unfortunately, many professionals who treat vaginismus patients—vulvovaginal specialists, gynecologists, sex therapists, psychologists, physical therapists, etc.—are unfamiliar with the Lamont classification system. Perhaps if Emily had suffered from Level 1 or

Level 2 vaginismus, she could have relaxed enough to progress with physical therapy, or another frequently prescribed technique that uses progressive dilation to stretch the vaginal muscles. Yet even Level 2 patients often have difficultly advancing with dilators on their own because of their inability to relax. In fact, I have many patients who gave up on dilators after one or more years of failure to progress. Once you get into Level 3 or Level 4, this kind of effort is often a lost cause in patients like Emily.

In many cases, a woman with Level 4 vaginismus may buy dilators, but she can't even bring herself to open the box. She may be committed to counseling, but virtually unable to incorporate the suggestions provided. It's also not uncommon for such a patient to cancel counseling sessions at the last moment, and feel physically ill on the day of therapy.

Given that Level 4 patients have such a strong aversion to any form of vaginal penetration or physical examination, it strikes me how much courage and willpower these women demonstrate when they even attempt pelvic floor physical therapy or other treatments.

If you are a vaginismus sufferer, I recommend that you assess the level of severity of your condition, using the Lamont classification table included in this chapter. If you determine that you are a Lamont Level 3 or above, this is not reason for despair, but it is information you should communicate to your doctor or therapist. This level of severity suggests you may need a more aggressive approach to treatment.

By using vaginal Botox injections and inserting a dilator under anesthesia (explained in the next section of this book), I see patients obtain fast and dramatic improvement. Vaginismus sufferers who previously could not tolerate being touched are able to self dilate to the largest dilator within three hours after their procedure. They continue to self dilate the next day even after the long-acting local anesthetic has worn off, and before the Botox has taken effect. Some may even allow their partner to assist in dilating.

It is always uplifting to witness how quickly a woman with Level 4 vaginismus—a level that is virtually impossible to address effectively with traditional methods—shifts to a much more treatable Level 1 or 2 vaginismus on the same day as the procedure. Three patients diagnosed at Level 4 were able to achieve intercourse on the day after their treatment, well before the Botox even had a chance to work, indicating the power of dilation under anesthesia and supervised dilation in the recovery room. An increasing number of patients are achieving intercourse in less than a week.

References:

1. Lamont, J.A. "Vaginismus." *American Journal of Obstetrics and Gynecology* 131 (1978): 633-6.

BREAKING DOWN THE WALL

A COMPREHENSIVE TREATMENT PROGRAM

A vaginismus patient who walks through the doors of my practice in Manchester, New Hampshire, has typically spent considerable time and effort attempting to overcome this condition already. It is often difficult for her to obtain an accurate diagnosis, given how relatively few doctors and therapists are even familiar with vaginismus. Or she may have sought treatment from a specialist who routinely assists vaginismus patients, but her case may be so severe that the treatment was unsuccessful.

Treatment approaches recommended by medical providers may fall short for severe cases of vaginismus because they do not address both the physical and psychological components of the condition. One of the main factors preventing women from having pain-free penetration is vaginal muscles spasms, but most programs are unable to address that facet of this condition.

For example, one frequently recommended treatment approach—progressive dilation—sometimes does not work for women with severe vaginismus. The goal of progressive dilation is to gradually stretch the vaginal wall, similar to the way you need to stretch a tight muscle before exercise, by inserting a series of dilators of increasing size. This process not only stretches the vaginal wall, but it is also intended to help the patient become more comfortable with the process of penetration because she is in control and can pace herself accordingly.

This practice of treating vaginismus through progressive dilation can be quite effective. But here is the problem: For women with severe vaginismus, the vagina is like a clenched fist, so trying to insert a dilator before it is unclenched is often a losing proposition, or may even reinforce the problem, given how slow and painful this process can be. Even without the issue of the physical barrier to dilation, the will may be there, but the hand guiding the dilator just can't follow through.

In many ways, the challenges of overcoming vaginismus are analogous to the old chicken-or-the-egg mystery. Which came first: the psychological issues that may have brought on the vaginal muscle spasms in the first place, or vaginal muscle spasms that first instill and then reinforce fear and phobic reactions to penetration? That conundrum is in part what makes this condition so devastating to women who want to enjoy painless intercourse and sexual pleasure.

Regardless of the answer to that question, it is sometimes necessary to provide a treatment approach that simultaneously addresses both the physical and psychological components of vaginismus. Over the last several years, we have developed a program that incorporates some of the more traditional approaches to overcoming vaginismus—dilation and supportive counseling—with new treatment protocols, including the use of Botox and dilation under anesthesia. In concert, this program addresses both the physical and psychological challenges of this condition head-on.

Most notably, the program includes a thirty-minute procedure in which Botox, a drug that temporarily prevents nerve impulses from reaching targeted muscles, is injected into the vaginal muscles to eliminate spasms. This procedure is performed while the patient is under a light form of general anesthesia, administered by an American Board of Anesthesiology (ABA) certified anesthesiologist. The anesthesiologist monitors and adjusts the level of anesthesia for each patient, depending on the level of spasms and how the patient is reacting.

At the end of the procedure, while the patient is still under anesthesia, a series of progressively larger dilators are inserted until the vagina is stretched sufficiently to accommodate a full-size dilator, where it remains after the patient regains consciousness. Patients become fully conscious almost immediately after the procedure, and they are typically able to transfer themselves from the operating table to the stretcher that brings them back to the recovery room.

Three Aspects to Treatment

1. Same-day procedure of vaginal Botox injections and dilator insertion, under sedation.

2. In-office dilation training and coaching.

3. At-home progressive dilation and supportive follow-up.

The combination of the Botox and indwelling dilator has resulted in a positive breakthrough for the treatment of vaginismus. The Botox, which typically goes into effect within two to seven days, eliminates vaginal spasm, a major physical impediment to penetration. In turn, the indwelling dilator "flips a psychological switch" for the patient. The dilator demonstrates to the patient that she is capable of comfortable penetration. The indwelling dilator also provides a jump-start to the process of progressive dilation that follows.

It bears noting that, due to the use of a local and topical anesthetic during the procedure, the dilator is not painful. Some patients state that having the dilator inside them feels "weird." Others report a mild discomfort or burning sensation, similar to the way a tight muscle aches after overuse during sports. This type of discomfort may occur during the first few days or weeks of working with dilators, as the formerly clenched vaginal muscles gradually become stretched.

Patients have had remarkable success after undergoing this procedure and following our treatment program. Patients dilate for two to three days according to a consistent schedule, and they also sleep with a medium sized dilator to achieve lengthy periods of dilation. On the third day after the procedure, patients are able to easily tolerate a finger examination, without the benefit of any anesthetic or drugs. For women who previously had never been able to experience any kind of vaginal examination without panic and great discomfort, this progress is indeed significant!

Much Gain…No Pain
The Purpose and Power of Anesthesia

Many prospective vaginismus patients naturally have questions about the use of anesthesia during the procedure. Sedation is necessary in large part to allow the examination and Botox injections, given that most women with vaginismus cannot even tolerate gentle touching. However, the anesthesia also serves other purposes, among them eradicating pain and controlling anxiety and fear. Dr. Richard Spaulding, an anesthesiologist who frequently works with me to treat vaginismus patients, explained how his pharmacologic plan targets all three of these factors.

"Some patients mistakenly perceive anesthesia as a loss of control," Dr. Spaulding clarified, "but that's not the case. Anxiety is often trying to take control of these patients and their behavior. We have medications that specifically target anxiety. They are powerful and fast-acting. After these medications are employed, most patients describe feeling more in control because they are not competing with their anxiety. Equally rapid and powerful medications exist to negate pain and blunt awareness. These are delivered in doses specific to each patient."

Dr. Spaulding continued, "Two phrases that I often find useful in conversing with anxious patients during their preoperative assessment are 'Sometimes, your imagination is not your friend,' and 'Name your fear.' Facts, clearly and calmly stated, can go a long way to defray stress. A fear that can be identified can be defused head on."

Typical Patient Questions
before Treatment in Our Surgi-Center

Q: Okay, so I'm going to be a patient. What can I expect?
A: Respect, honesty, and caring. The healing starts now.

Q: Will I be listened to?
A: Absolutely, and you will be heard. We want to answer your questions. We want to know how you are doing.

Q: How do you manage my pain?
A: Actively and preemptively. Pain medications are administered during anesthesia. Local anesthetics in the form of long-acting numbing medicines are administered in the treated area. Post-treatment pain medications are prescribed to accommodate your specific needs.

Q: Will I be safe?
A: Safety is paramount. Our surgical center has had continuous certification since 1985. You will be monitored and observed by trained personnel throughout your procedure. Modern outpatient anesthesia is safer per minute than operating a motor vehicle, just to offer a comparison activity.

Q: How can I help the people that want to help me?
A: Prepare before arriving for your procedure. Read and follow your written instructions. Review your personal health history, including allergies, surgeries, medications, and over-the-counter agents you use. Ask about anything that concerns you. If you have any remaining questions, write them down if it helps you to remember them. Communicate how medications are or are not making you feel. Provide feedback.

But Will I Be Able to Have Sex?

One of the first questions potential patients ask is: "What is your success rate in treating this condition?" This question is understandable, as many of these women do not want to invest in more false hope. Many of them must travel great distances to receive treatment; we have worked with patients from countries throughout the world. For those women who are facing relationship issues because of this condition, or who are eager to start families, the clock is ticking. They want a real solution, a real cure.

I am happy to report that, during my first five years performing the procedure, more than 90 percent of the vaginismus patients who have come to me were able to have intercourse within one week to four months. Examples of patients who have not been able to achieve intercourse were a Lamont Level 5 patient who was never able to tolerate any form of penetration, and was unable to progress beyond the smallest dilator; a Level 4 patient who was able to advance to the largest dilator, but not to intercourse; and another Level 4 patient who did not have enough time to dilate in the days following her procedure and took eight months to achieve intercourse. In the last two cases, there were some relationship issues and/or a partner's erectile dysfunction that appeared to have played a role in the slower progress.

When it is reported that more than 90 percent of the vaginismus patients are cured, the term "cure" is being defined as the ability to achieve pain-free penetration. But perhaps the term is best expressed in the following journal entry from a former patient who was diagnosed with the most severe form of vaginismus.

On day 51 after Ginny received the Botox injections and indwelling dilator, she wrote: "We had sex again last night and it was the best ever! I was uncomfortable at the start like always, but we quickly found a very good position and I could easily ignore the stretching on the outside. Sex even started to feel good and I was brave enough to move instead of just lying still. I am really starting to feel normal for the first time ever!"

As a postscript, Ginny continued to dilate consistently in the months that followed this missive, and she was able to achieve comfortable and pleasurable intercourse.

Overcoming Your Vaginismus: Step by Step

The following provides a brief overview of my treatment program, and the remaining chapters in this section will elaborate more fully on the procedures and practices used to treat vaginismus patients. As an FYI to clinicians reading this book: In an effort to make this program available to more women around the world, I welcome colleagues to come to my office to observe the procedure and train with my team.

Pre-procedure assessment. Every patient completes a pre-procedure questionnaire and personal health history forms to provide us with a detailed history of her condition, such as previous treatments, family and medical history, religious upbringing, stresses, sexual history, and gynecological examinations. Patients are asked to rate the severity of their pain and associated fear using the Lamont classification of vaginismus. We also request records or a summary statement from recent health care providers who have treated the patient for this condition. We then review this information and thoroughly discuss the details by telephone, Skype, or an in-office consultation.

Anesthesia evaluation. The day of the procedure, the patient changes into a hospital gown and settles into a comfortable, heated bed in our recovery room. We administer Valium about thirty minutes before her examination to help with relaxation. Every patient is then evaluated by an ABA-certified anesthesiologist who starts her on an intravenous drip. For patients who are uncomfortable with needles, nitrous oxide can be used to alleviate any fear. In such instances, the intravenous drip will be started in the operating room.

External examination and testing for vulvar disorders. By the time the patient is brought to the operating room the Valium has usually taken effect. For patients who are nervous, additional sedation is given intravenously. I then conduct an external examination to determine if there are any associated problems. A Q-Tip test is then performed to determine if there is associated vulvodynia or vestibulodynia. There is no attempt to perform an internal examination at this time.

Internal examination. Additional sedation is delivered in the form of Monitored Anesthesia Care (MAC), a light form of general anesthesia in which no breathing tube is required. Once the patient is sedated and comfortable, I perform a digital internal examination to determine the exact location and severity of the spasms. The examination is also used to determine how much Botox is necessary, as well as the location in which it should be injected. To offset the possibility of any pain, my gloved finger is coated with a topical anesthetic, 2 percent Xylocaine jelly mixed with Surgilube. A speculum examination is done to rule out associated problems and confirm the normal length, width, and compliance of the vagina. I also examine the hymenal ring.

Botox injections. Tiny, delicate needles deliver the Botox to the targeted muscles. The injections are located along the lateral (side) walls of the vagina, and care is taken to avoid the area below the urethra and the area in contact with the rectum. Following the Botox injections, I inject a long-acting local anesthetic, Sensorcaine, which lasts about six to twelve hours, to further alleviate any post-procedure discomfort.

Intraoperative dilation. At the end of the procedure, which takes about thirty minutes, I perform progressive dilation of the vagina. I begin the process using a medium #4 size dilator, and I then progress to the larger #5 dilator. The vagina is then dilated to the largest dilator, #6, which is left in place. Even the larger dilators are easily inserted due to the fact that the vagina is completely relaxed at this point. The patient's partner is often in the operating room during the procedure and is encouraged to assist with the dilation process. The partner's participation is important because the sooner he is involved in the dilation process, the more comfortable the couple will become as they work together towards penetration.

Waking up with the dilator. The patient is awake almost immediately after the procedure, and she is transferred to the recovery room. The first moments of consciousness prove to be both emotional and triumphant for every patient, as she realizes that she is already experiencing pain-free penetration with a large dilator. For most patients, this is the first time penetration has ever been possible.

Supervised dilation, counseling, and confidence building. During the two days following the procedure, patients and their partners, if applicable, spend about three to four hours relaxing in the recovery room each morning while receiving instructions for dilation therapy. While they are advancing with the dilators, they are counseled on how to eventually transition from dilators to intercourse.

As mentioned earlier, some of my patients, and sometimes even their partners, do not know where the vagina is located. Therefore, we provide an anatomy lesson, holding a mirror between the patient's legs as she works with the dilators. These sessions help to establish a neutral or positive relationship between a patient and her vagina, which in the past may have been negative or even physically nauseating.

Our office also encourages vaginismus patients, who receive treatment the same day, to become acquainted while they are in the recovery area. This component of the program is completely voluntary, but we have found it to be useful because it provides a sense of community and a support network for women who have too long felt isolated because of this condition.

On the final day, we usually conduct a round-table discussion with the patients who have been treated and their partners. We answer any remaining questions, and provide a final review of their dilation schedule. This is one of my favorite parts of the treatment program. By this point, patients are elated with their rapid progress with dilation, and feel empowered to continue. Their smiles speak volumes about how much they have already achieved.

Ongoing coaching. The Botox becomes effective in two to seven days and normally lasts about four months. This time frame provides an adequate period for our patients to progressively dilate in order to stretch their vaginal muscles, and to transition to intercourse while the Botox is still in effect. Throughout this process, we stay in close communication with patients to monitor their progress, answer questions, and to offer advice on sexuality issues. During this time frame, some patients also choose to work with a professional therapist to address issues of intimacy.

Sexual functioning follow-up. We follow our patients' progress for one or more years after the procedure using questionnaires, including the Female Sexual Function Index (FSFI). We foster regular communication and updates with all of our patients, and consider them part of our growing "family." When relevant, we continue to communicate with the patients' other healthcare professionals who are providing complementary treatment or therapy for issues related to vaginismus.

BOTOX FOR VAGINISMUS:
THE MISSING LINK?

I n 2005 Angela, age 23, contacted my practice to ask whether
I would treat her vaginismus using Botox injections. She explained
that she had experienced pain with intercourse since her first sexual
experience at age 16. She had tried lubricants, numbing agents,
muscle relaxants, anti-anxiety medications, physical therapy, counseling
with sex therapists, and therapy with dilators, but nothing really helped.

Angela had been with her boyfriend for seven years, but was unable
to have intercourse with him unless she went "unconscious" through the
use of either alcohol or medications. After intercourse, she remembered
nothing. Her boyfriend had become increasingly frustrated about having
sex under these conditions. I later met him when he accompanied Angela
to an appointment. He told me privately that he experienced no satisfaction when they had sex, and it had become simply a form of release.

Angela had contacted me because she had read about a new
treatment for vaginismus that involved Botox injections in the vaginal
muscles. She was nervous about the procedure but was unwilling to give
up on her dreams of having "normal" sex, and she hoped that this might
be the solution.

Angela's story moved me deeply. This woman was clearly suffering.
I admired how thoroughly she had done her homework, researching
treatment options, and learning almost everything about a condition

that, to this day, is often overlooked in gynecology programs. Angela had reached out to me because she knew that I had successfully been giving patients Botox injections for cosmetic purposes for years. Her cry for help ultimately changed the course of my practice.

....

I never was able to insert a dilator alone. Just the tip. So after one year working with a man gynecologist, I started another treatment with a woman gynecologist. She was so good to me. We had two-hour sessions per week, and we worked on a sofa! Yay! She was there with me, with all the patience in the world, saying, "C'mon, a little more in, a little more in." In three months, I was doing the bigger size dilator. But I had a problem. I needed around an hour and a half to insert the bigger dilators, and that is very bad because the penis cannot wait so much time. :) My muscles were really tight, and my fear was huge too. So I decided to do the Botox, and now I can insert the dilators in few minutes!!!
– a vaginismus patient who came from Europe for treatment

....

Botox to Prevent Spasm

Botox is the trade name for an injectable neurotoxin—Botulinum Toxin Type A—manufactured by Allergan, Inc., a company located in Irvine, California. A small dose of the drug, injected into a targeted muscle, temporarily prevents nerve impulses from reaching that muscle by interfering with the release of acetylcholine, a chemical needed to activate the muscle. Botox is commonly used to erase the furrows or frown lines between eyebrows that typically develop as we age. Botox does not cause numbness but it does prevent muscles from contracting. It usually takes between two to seven days for the injected drug to take effect, and remains effective for approximately four months.

But Botox for vaginismus?

In truth, I had never even heard of vaginismus in medical school or in my decades of practice. I was intrigued to learn more about using Botox to treat this disorder, but my research at the time uncovered only two references in the scientific literature. The first article involved a case study conducted in 1997, in which a patient with secondary vaginismus was treated with Botox injections in her vaginal muscles. She subsequently was able to have intercourse for the first time in eight years, and the results persisted over the entire twenty-four months that the patient was followed in the study.

The only other article I found was published in 2004 by two doctors in Iran. The article described the use of botulinum toxin in a group of twenty-four vaginismus patients. This study used the drug Dysport, a type of botulinum neurotoxin, BoNTA-ABO, commonly used in Europe and produced by Ipsen Ltd., United Kingdom. It received FDA approval in 2009. The Dysport was injected into the pelvic floor muscles outside the vagina between the vagina and anus. Twenty-three of the women treated were able to have vaginal examinations one week after the procedure, at which time they had little or no remaining signs of vaginismus.

I was encouraged after reading about these cases, and I notified Angela that I would attempt to treat her vaginismus with Botox. While it was premature to become too excited about Botox as a cure-all for this condition, the treatment method nonetheless seemed logical. Botox injections are commonly associated with cosmetic procedures; however the medication also has a variety of therapeutic uses.

Botox has been used for decades to weaken over-active muscles and glands. For example, it is regularly used to control muscular spasms in patients with cerebral palsy and stroke. Botox is also effective in the treatment of migraine headaches, excessive sweating, Raynaud's Disease (a disorder causing spasm of the blood vessels of the extremities), and many other conditions that produce muscle contractions. Given the primary physical symptom of vaginismus—involuntary spasms of the vaginal muscles—this new application for this drug seemed well worth a try. What's more, most physicians agree that when Botox is properly administered, it is as safe as many common medicines, such as aspirin. It has very few side effects and a wide margin of safety.

Success on a Trial Basis

As my first vaginismus patient, Angela proved to be both a success story and a learning experience. She received a measured injection of

Botox along each lateral side of her vaginal muscles. Botox injections are normally given without any anesthesia, but Angela, like most vaginismus patients, required sedation because of the amount of fear associated with any kind of vaginal examination or contact. Angela woke up quickly from the anesthesia and there were no complications. The entire procedure took about thirty minutes.

The Botox prevented Angela's vaginal muscles from going into spasm, and during the time period the injections remained effective she worked with progressively larger dilators to stretch the muscles of her vagina. This ongoing dilation, in conjunction with the relaxed muscle tone of the vagina, plays a crucial role in easing the transition to intercourse. About three months after her Botox procedure, Angela achieved pain-free intercourse for the first time in her life. Since then, she has reported no setbacks.

As I continued to use Botox to treat other vaginismus patients, I eventually determined that I had actually undertreated Angela. I had used a very low dose of Botox during that first case because I thought it necessary to maintain some vaginal tone. In retrospect, the lower dose only slowed the treatment program, while providing no safety or other benefits. (Note: As the effect of the Botox wears off over a span of four to six months, normal vaginal tone returns to all patients.)

With experience, I began to observe the value of using higher doses of Botox, generally 150 units, to eliminate wider areas of vaginal spasm. I also began to inject both Botox and a long-acting local anesthetic, Bupivacaine, into all three of the muscles that make up the muscular wall of the vagina to the level of the cervix, rather than only treating the entry muscle of the vagina. These modifications to the procedure were developed after one patient's indwelling dilator dropped into the toilet shortly after her procedure. I had failed to treat the spasms of her puborectalis or mid-vaginal muscle, and she had experienced considerable difficulty reinserting the dilator.

I have continued to make refinements to the procedure over the past several years. Our treatment program for vaginismus now includes both the use of Botox injections, as well as progressive dilation under anesthesia. Patients currently wake up from the procedure with a large dilator coated with topical anesthesia inside them, allowing them to immediately experience pain-free penetration. The use of an indwelling dilator has reduced the time between treatment and intercourse from

tely three months to a few weeks, or, in some cases, a matter
also seems to provide the psychological "jump-start" that is
to overcome the fear of penetration.

Rethinking the Treatment of Last Resort

I have been amazed by the profound results that I have observed
using Botox and dilation under anesthesia to treat vaginismus. This drug,
which is commonly known for removing wrinkles, may be the "missing
link" when it comes to providing a rapid cure for women with severe
cases of vaginismus. Botox nonetheless remains a relatively unknown
and under-used form of treatment for vaginismus, even though it has
been used to treat this condition since 1997. To date, the use of Botox
for vaginismus has been reported in less than two hundred cases. The
relatively few medical providers who know about this application often
consider Botox the treatment of last resort for vaginismus.

My use of Botox for vaginismus is outlined in a research paper I
published in 2009, which describes my experience treating twenty vaginismus patients from 2005 to 2009. Twelve of these women had primary
vaginismus with symptoms that merited a determination of the most
severe Lamont Level 4 vaginismus; five of the women had secondary
vaginismus, meaning they had been able to have intercourse at some
point previously; and three patients had severe dyspareunia (painful
intercourse).

After receiving Botox injections and working with progressively
larger dilators (progressive dilation is covered in depth in chapter 11),
sixteen of these women were able to achieve intercourse within two
weeks to three months. Three of the other patients progressed to the
largest dilators and were later able to advance to intercourse after the
study was published.

One patient, after success with the larger dilators, subsequently
regressed to the smallest size and was unable to advance any further.
Although she had progressed from her previous inability to tolerate any
form of penetration, I still considered this case a "failure" in my study. I
also had another patient with secondary vaginismus who experienced two
recurrences of vaginismus. However, each time she was able to overcome
the condition by getting back on track with a dilation schedule.

In my trial, the women treated with Botox for their vaginismus reported no complications. One patient experienced the side effect of excessive vaginal dryness, which was likely caused by the Botox because it blocks the parasympathetic nervous system that governs vaginal lubrication. The other patients who used lubrication did not notice any dryness. None of my patients have had any urinary or fecal incontinence.

These findings, and the results of the other early studies, suggest that the use of Botox may be the difference between success and failure when it comes to treating vaginismus. If nothing else, it shortens the time of treatment and provides an effective "relapse intervention." As the vaginal muscles begin to relax after the Botox takes effect, patients previously suffering from Level 4 vaginismus quickly drop to a Level 1 or 2. Once the vaginal spasms are eliminated, they become more willing and able to work with dilators to stretch the muscles. They also become more comfortable with this part of their body and tend to improve overall vaginal hygiene. As a result, the act of penetration becomes easier both physically and psychologically.

I am aware that more research needs to be conducted on Botox for vaginismus, and that other modalities may prove to be more effective in the future. Moreover, although the use of Botox successfully weakens the vaginal muscles to prevent spasms, it does not automatically alleviate the fear of penetration. For those reasons, Botox in combination with the insertion of an indwelling dilator under anesthesia, as well as ongoing support during the dilation process post procedure, is crucial to success.

I was reminded again of the importance of combining all aspects of a comprehensive treatment program, after speaking to a woman with severe vaginismus who had recently undergone vaginal Botox injections at a different practice. Her treatment did not include any post procedure dilation or follow-up counseling. The result: a month without progress. It was only after she was treated again, this time with dilation under anesthesia and ongoing support, that she started making progress.

This case reinforces the fact that Botox injections are not a magic bullet that can, on their own, eliminate all cases of vaginismus. However, for patients like Angela and all the other women with Lamont Level 3 or 4 vaginismus who have tried everything from working with dila-tors, to taking drugs or drinking themselves into a stupor, to undergoing surgical procedures, this so-called "last resort" of treatment appears to mark a real advancement in breaking down that immutable "wall" that makes sex seem impossible.

Studies on the Use of Botox
for Vaginismus and Vulvodynia

Since 1997 a number of articles have been published describing the use of Botox for more severe cases of vaginismus. My own study was published in the December 2009 issue of *Plastic and Reconstructive Surgery*. In addition, numerous publications can be found involving theories and treatment of vulvodynia. Here too, Botox is becoming more accepted for refractory cases, cases resistant to treatment.

1997: An early report on the use of Botox for secondary vaginismus was reported as a case history by Brin and Vapnek.[1] The patient was initially treated with only 10 units of Botox, a small dose, and later with an additional 40 units of Botox. This patient was able to have intercourse for the first time in eight years. The results persisted for the 24 months of follow-up.

2000: In a controlled study from Egypt, eight women were injected with 50 units of Botox for vaginismus into the bulbospongiosus muscles, and five matched women injected with saline. All women given Botox were able to have intercourse, whereas the controls did not improve during a follow up period of 10.2 +/- 3.3 months. Of the patients given Botox, none required re-injection and there was no recurrence or complication during the follow-up period.[2]

2004: Ghazizadeh and Nikzad[3] in Iran reported on the use of botulinum toxin in the treatment of refractory vaginismus at level 3 and 4, in twenty-four patients. In this study, Dysport in the amount of 150-400 mIU was used. Twenty-three patients were able to have vaginal examinations one week post procedure showing little or no vaginismus. One patient refused vaginal examination and did not attempt intercourse. Of the twenty-three patients, eighteen (75 percent) achieved satisfactory intercourse, four (17 percent) had mild pain, and one patient was unable to have intercourse because of her husband's impotence. A second dose of Dysport was needed on one patient.

2006: Abbott et al[4] reported results from a double-blinded, randomized, controlled and statistically analyzed study to evaluate chronic pain and pelvic floor spasm. Sixty patients were divided into two groups of thirty each, one group receiving 80 units of Botulinum Toxin A injected into the pelvic floor muscles, and the other group receiving saline as a placebo. Pelvic floor pressures measured by vaginal manometry were noted to be significantly improved in the Botulinum Toxin Type A group.

2006: Yoon, et al[5] reported on seven patients using Botox for the treatment of vulvodynia. After determining the exact pain sites with a cotton tip and gentle digital palpation, injections were given into the vestibule (four patients), levator ani muscle (two patients), and the perineal body (one patient). Initially, 20 units of Botox were used which gave relief in two patients. The other five patients received a second dose of 40 units two weeks later with considerable improvement in their pain scores. No recurrences were noted during a twenty-four-month follow-up period. The patients treated had varying degrees of painful intercourse due to their vulvodynia; none were noted to have vaginismus.

2009: My study, published in the December issue of *Plastic and Reconstructive Surgery* showed a success rate of more than 90 percent. In this study of my first twenty patients, most with severe vaginismus, a treatment program was developed consisting of intravaginal injections of Botox, a long-acting local anesthetic and progressive dilation under anesthesia.[6] By July 2010, over seventy patients had been treated for vaginismus. Two patients had vaginal delivery of normal children. One of these patients had a miscarriage with her first pregnancy due to low hormones. Another patient miscarried soon after conceiving for unknown reasons. At the time of this writing three patients are enjoying healthy pregnancies.

After Angela received treatment in December 2005, another fourteen months passed before I was contacted by another woman with vaginismus. My second vaginismus patient also experienced positive results from the intravaginal Botox injections. I then successfully treated a third patient three months later. With each case, my interest in treating this condition and my excitement about finding a real "cure" grew. Positive results, and knowing what a difference this approach has made in the lives of these women, have motivated me to devote a significant part of my plastic surgery practice to the treatment of vaginismus. I also continue to conduct research to refine my treatment program, write articles about the condition for professional publications, and offer information and testimonials through my practice's website.

I have now treated almost one hundred women diagnosed with vaginismus, and receive one or two inquiries a day from women with this condition. These women frequently find me by performing their own research on the Internet, similar to the way Angela and I connected. The success rate in treating this condition remains over 90 percent. I continue to follow the progress of most of the women I have treated. I am heartened by all their stories of freedom from the fear of penetration… of consummating their relationships…and of becoming moms!

"I can't tell you how glad I am I made the decision to use Botox," wrote one of my earliest patients. "It changed my life completely. All the stress and frustration my husband and I went through are gone. By allowing us to enjoy a good sexual relationship, Botox helped restore equilibrium, trust, and happiness in our marriage. And most importantly, it allowed me to experience the wonderful joy of motherhood! Now, thanks to the Botox, I have built a family. And I am planning to expand it soon with another child!"

Everything You Always Wanted to Know about Botox

Below are answers to common questions many patients have about Botox.

Q: How safe is Botox?
A: Botox has a long track record of considerable safety and is probably safer than aspirin when properly used. Botox is the trade name for a drug that is derived from a strain of bacteria called Botulinum. This is the

same neurotoxic protein responsible for the disease botulism, hence there has been concern and misunderstanding related to its safety. Though Botulinum Toxin Type A is highly toxic, the amounts used for cosmetic and medical purposes to weaken or partially paralyze unwanted activity in spastic muscles are diluted to a high level of safety. It is estimated that it would take 200 vials to cause illness. For vaginismus, 150 units—or 1.5 vials of Botox—is all that is required.

First approved for clinical use by eye doctors in 1981 to treat spasm of the eyelid muscles, Botox has a long history of safety and efficacy, and was approved by the FDA for cosmetic purposes in 2002. Botox for vaginismus was first used in 1997. FDA approval is pending for this particular application as well as many others, and, therefore, Botox is considered an "off label" drug in the treatment of vaginismus. This means physicians can use it if there is a reasonable expectation that the patient will be helped.

Q: I'd like to get pregnant. Is this safe after the Botox procedure?
A: Millions of injections used worldwide for a variety of conditions have shown no evidence of it being harmful to a developing fetus. Nevertheless, it is always a good idea to avoid drugs in general when contemplating a pregnancy. Congenital malformations can occur and, by avoiding drugs at the time of conception, there is one less worry about a particular drug causing an unexpected problem. Since the effects of Botox last about four to six months, we request patients use birth control during this time interval.

Q: Can Botox cause miscarriage?
A: There is no implication of Botox causing miscarriages. It is important to note that roughly 30 percent of first-time pregnancies result in a miscarriage, usually due to fetal problems. By waiting four to six months until the Botox is out of your system, there are fewer worries about getting pregnant.

Q: Are there any side effects to Botox?
A: Botox interferes with the parasympathetic nervous symptom, which delivers lubrication to the vagina. The result can be vaginal dryness. Accordingly, it is important for women who have had vaginal Botox injections to use lots of lubrication during intercourse.

Q: Is it possible to have orgasms during the three to four months the Botox is in effect?

A: Yes. Orgasms are possible during this time and can be quite satisfying. Patients have commented that their orgasms feel different after the Botox wears off and they can better experience vaginal contractions. This difference could also be attributed to the fact that after three to four months of intercourse they have become more comfortable with their sexuality and less inhibited.

Q: Given that the effects of Botox are temporary, will I need more vaginal injections later to re-treat my vaginismus so I can continue to have pain-free intercourse?

A: Because Botox begins to wear off at about four months, it's best to complete the transition from dilators to intercourse within that time frame. Once this happens, however, it's unlikely that you will need additional Botox because both your body and your mind will have already learned the important lesson that it is possible to insert something painlessly into your vagina. This one-time application of Botox for vaginismus is in contrast to the use of Botox for other conditions, which typically require repeat injections every three to four months. (Note: intercourse is not a substitute for dilation, which should be continued for three months to a year following the Botox treatment.)

Q: Can Botox be used for other pain disorders involving the genitalia?

A: Recent studies are showing Botox to be a highly successful treatment not only for vaginismus, but also vulvodynia (pain involving some part of the vulva), and vestibulodynia (a form of vulvodynia in which the pain is located in the vestibule just outside the vagina). The reason Botox may be effective in these different medical conditions is because the drug not only relaxes muscular activity, but also has a direct effect on pain.

Q: If Botox works for vaginismus, vulvodynia, and other pain disorders, why is it important to distinguish these medical conditions when treating them?

A: It's important because the question that must be asked is, "Is it the vaginismus and spasm of the vaginal muscles causing pain with intercourse, or is it the vestibulodynia that causes the pain?" Even though Botox seems to work for both conditions, the doctor needs to know whether to inject the Botox to the spastic muscles of the vagina, the vestibule, or the vulva.

Q: Is Botox in the treatment of vaginismus covered by insurai

A: In the most recent version of the *Diagnostic and Statistic (DSM-IV)*, published by the American Psychiatric As vaginismus is classified as a sexual pain disorder. Given this ῀ ...., the treatment of vaginismus with Botox may be covered by insurance. Patients should contact their health insurance carriers for further information about their personal policies.

References:

1. Brin, M.F. and J.M. Vapnek. "Treatment of vaginismus with botulinum toxin injections." *Lancet* 349 (1997): 252-253.
2. Shafik A. and O. El-Sibai. "Vaginismus: results of treatment with Botulin Toxin." *Journal of Obstetrics and Gynaecology* 20 (2000): 300-2
3. Ghazizadeh, S. and M. Nikzad. "Botulinum Toxin in the Treatment of Refractory Vaginismus." *Journal of Obstetrics and Gynaecology* 104 (2004): 922-925.
4. Abbott, J.A.; Jarvis, S.K.; Lyons, S.D.; Thomson, A. and T.G. Vancaille. "Botulinum Toxin Type A for chronic pain and pelvic floor spasm in women: a randomized controlled trial." *Journal of Obstetrics and Gynaecology* 108 (2006): 915-923.
5. Yoon, H.; Chung, W.S. and B.S. Shim. "Botulinum Toxin A for the management of vulvodynia." *International Journal of Impotence Research* 19 (2007): 84-87.
6. Pacik, P.T. "Viewpoint: Botox treatment for vaginismus." *Plastic Surgery & Reconstructive Surgery* 24 (2009): 455e-456e.

Behind the Scenes in the Surgi-Center: One Woman's Procedure

The heart monitor beeps steadily in the surgi-center as 31-year-old Maria is placed under anesthesia. Soft music is playing in the background. As Maria lies on the operating room table, she looks even smaller than her 5-foot, 97-pound frame. Small amounts of medications, in this case Propofol, Versed, and Fentanyl, run through her intravenous tube. The drugs induce sedation and control pain. In fact, Propofol is sometimes referred to as "milk of amnesia" because a patient forgets what happens while this white liquid is administered.

Maria's boyfriend, Stephen, is holding her hand, his scrubs somewhat short for his six-foot, four-inch frame. Stephen is in the operating room for the same reason the boyfriends and husbands of many of my patients make this journey—they want to support their loved ones.

Maria and Stephen have been dating for over four years, but they have never had intercourse. They have been on the verge of breaking up because of this obstacle. He loves her, but wants to start a family. The stress of trying and failing to have sex for so many years has taken its toll on these two people, individually and as a couple.

Maria rests quietly as the fluid flows through her intravenous tube. The beep of the heart monitor remains steady; not too fast, not too slow. This is good. In her "everyday" life, Maria neither smokes nor drinks, but she takes medication for high blood pressure.

Maria is monitored closely by the anesthesiologist, operating room nurse, and myself. It is vital that she is monitored closley because anesthesia affects the blood flow. Maria has had previous allergic reactions to certain antibiotics, and she also has a history of a heart murmur. The readout on her heart monitor shows a pulse of 82, a blood pressure of 120 over 80, normal oxygen saturation, and a normal ECG, all signs that the procedure is a go.

Dr. Rick Spaulding, an American board certified anesthesiologist, devotes his full concentration to the intravenous medications to control Maria's level of sedation. Dr. Spaulding is on staff at a nearby medical center, and we are fortunate to have him work with us, as well. He has a quiet demeanor, a good sense of humor, and a way of alleviating patients' fears about anesthetics and their unease at being in unfamiliar surroundings. In addition to his young family and racing cars, Dr. Spaulding's work is his passion and it shows in the care he provides every patient.

Dr. Spaulding nods to indicate to me that I can start the procedure. Ellen, our surgical technician, is already preparing the syringes of highly diluted Botox that I will inject intravaginally. Our other surgical technician, Pammy, stands next to me, ready to assist.

I do an external examination of Maria's vulva and conclude that everything looks normal. My gloved finger, coated with Surgilube and 2 percent Xylocaine jelly, is slowly and lightly introduced into her vagina to perform an internal examination. Maria noticeably resists and pulls back. She is completely asleep and her vital signs are stable, but somehow she knows she is not comfortable. I assure Stephen that she will not remember anything.

I indicate to Dr. Spaulding that Maria needs to be taken to a deeper level of sedation. I wait, keeping my gloved hands clasped to maintain sterility. I am not surprised by Maria's unease with vaginal contact, even when unconscious. Her inability to have any form of vaginal penetration, including tampons, dates back almost a decade, and may have taken root in a devastating incident. Maria shared with us earlier that, at age five, she was molested by a cousin, but only fully recalled the event years later in college when her boyfriend at the time tried to make her have sex. Since then, sexual penetration and gynecological examinations have been impossible for her.

Less than a minute after Maria's anesthetic has been increased, another nod from Dr. Spaulding tells me to continue my examination.

By now Maria has received 50mg of Propofol, 4mg of IV Versed, and 3 mg of Fentanyl, enough to fully sedate a two-hundred pound man.

Maria is still resisting. Examination reveals 4+/4 spasm of the bulbocavernosus entry muscle. Each muscle is examined separately and assigned a degree of spasm with 4 being the most severe. I can barely insert my index finger in her vagina.

I move aside so Stephen also can do an examination, which Maria has previously consented was permissible. One touch speaks volumes about what his girlfriend has been going through with this condition, allowing for an understanding that transcends words. Before proceeding, I ask Stephen if he is doing okay. He is a strong guy, and I'm sure familiar with pressure, given his job as a financial analyst. However, an operating room may be outside his comfort zone. More than one partner has had to leave during the procedure to gulp some fresh air.

Above the entry muscle is the pubococcygeus muscle (the PC muscle) responsible for the ability to do Kegel contractions of the pelvic floor. This is the muscle that automatically contracts when fighting a full bladder and the need to urinate. In both medical and nonscientific publications, the PC muscle has been implicated as the major muscle of spasm in vaginismus. With Maria, however, the PC muscles show only light spasm. This mirrors what I have seen in most of my vaginismus patients.

As I proceed with the examination, I am reminded yet again of the value of conducting it while the patient is sedated. This is the only way patients with severe vaginismus can tolerate an internal examination due to the degree of fear they experience. Allowing this examination also offers important insights about the mid-vagina, or puborectalis muscle. In Maria's case, the puborectalis muscle shows a level of 3+/4 spasm, slightly less in intensity than the spasm of her vagina's entry muscle. The puborectalis is usually the last barrier to achieving full intercourse in women who have spasm of this muscle. For some women, though not Maria, it is the only muscle in spasm, allowing them to achieve partial intercourse.

Ellen, the surgical technician, has already drawn up the Botox and hands me the syringe. I decide to inject a higher dose into the entry muscle, and divide the rest of the Botox into the remaining two muscles. As the Botox is injected intravaginally, the rhythm of the heart monitor continues to indicate that all is well. Maria's blood pressure has dipped slightly to 100/70, well within normal limits. ECG shows a normal sinus rhythm.

Injecting the Botox takes only a matter of minutes. Over the course of the procedure, I reflect on the long letter Marie wrote to her family several months ago, and shared with me and my staff. I read it last night and was moved by her honesty and willingness to provide a written account of her experience with vaginismus. Maria's letter describes her long and painful journey to overcome this condition, as well as her other issues relating to intimacy.

Maria has been seeing a counselor at Stephen's urging, her third one through the years. She feels therapy has helped her as far as being able to open up to some of her family regarding the molestation. Unfortunately, neither the therapy nor the counselor's suggestion that she try using a vibrator have helped her in actually having sex; she bought a vibrator, but couldn't bring herself to use it.

I glance at Stephen, still standing strong by his girlfriend's side. In the letter, Maria describes Stephen as "the man I felt God truly placed on this earth just for me." Yet, she also explains that whenever they have tried to have sex, she closes her thighs and pushes him back, to keep him from entering her body. It is hard to imagine these two breaking up, even though I know this is the toll that vaginismus can take on countless couples.

With the Botox injections complete, it is time to progress to the next phase of the procedure, which involves injecting a long-acting local anesthetic into the side walls of the vagina. This numbs the vagina so that the dilator cannot be felt. It also makes it easier for the patient to work with the dilators in the recovery room.

The procedure is concluded by inserting a series of progressively larger dilators into Maria's vagina to determine which size should remain in place when she wakes up in the recovery room. This process goes more easily than I expected, even though I can still detect some residual overall tightness of her vagina, despite the heavy dose of anesthesia.

Noting the persistence of these physical spasms, even when the patient is sedated, explains why some vaginismus patients like Maria are unable to obtain a successful outcome through the use of counseling, or at least not until the spasms are addressed.

"One to two minutes," I tell Dr. Spaulding, as I make the final determination of which size dilator will remain in place. I elect to have

Maria wake up with a #5 in her vagina. Because of its color, my staff has affectionately nicknamed this dilator Miss Pink. The #5 is one size smaller than the largest dilator, Mr. Big Blue.

Before asking Dr. Spaulding to bring Maria back to full consciousness, Stephen is shown how to insert the dilator into his girlfriend's vagina. The trick is to direct the tip of the dilator towards the rectum, before angling it upward for full insertion. This maneuver helps avoid the tip of the dilator from coming into contact with the cervix. Inserting the dilator this way will make it more comfortable for Maria when she continues to dilate daily over the coming weeks. Because Maria's vagina is too short for the full length of the dilator, about an inch of it projects out of her body, which is perfectly normal. Assuming that Maria remains comfortable with Stephen's participation, this shared activity of working with the dilators over the weeks to come will go a long way in establishing a new level of comfort, trust, and intimacy between them.

My assistants, Ellen and Pammy, help lower Maria's legs from the stirrups. She opens her eyes. At first she is dreamy, but quickly recognizes Stephen who, once again, has a firm grip on her hand. Maria will spend the rest of the morning in our recovery room, snuggling under an electric blanket and getting used to removing and re-inserting the dilator—her first experience with pain-free penetration!

Over the next two days, Maria and Stephen will return to our office to practice dilation under the supervision of our staff. This will help them gain the confidence and insights they need to continue the dilation process at home. We cannot emphasize enough the importance of regular dilation in order to stretch the vaginal muscles in preparation for intercourse.

But for now, as Maria easily comes back to full consciousness, our first job is to tell her how great she did. She wakes up, sees Stephen beside her, and a smile crosses her face.

Procedure Facts and Figures

 Botox injections for vaginismus require about a thirty-minute procedure, performed in an out-patient operating room or surgi-center, while the patient is under heavy sedation.

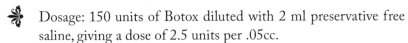 Dosage: 150 units of Botox diluted with 2 ml preservative free saline, giving a dose of 2.5 units per .05cc.

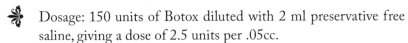 Area of injections: A medium size speculum keeps the vaginal canal open for a clear visual of the treatment area. A 1cc no-waste syringe with a one-inch, 30-gauge needle, slightly bent, is used to inject the Botox in multiple areas along each lateral side of the vagina, to include the bulbocavernosus, pubococcygeus, and puborectalis muscles, which are generally the areas of maximum spasm. The muscles are close to the lining of the vagina and therefore superficial injections under the mucosa are effective.

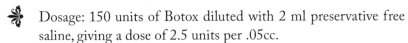 Local anesthetics: 20-30 ml of 0.25 percent bupivacaine with 1:400,000 epinephrine is injected into the lateral aspects of the same three muscles, again just below the vaginal mucosa, to create numbness for about six to twelve hours.

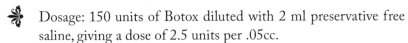 Progressive dilation: Dilators coated with 2 percent Lidocaine jelly, a topical anesthetic, mixed with Surgilube, are inserted in the vagina and one remains in place when the patient wakes up in recovery, allowing her to experience pain-free penetration, often for the first time in her life. At this point, most patients are able to tolerate the largest dilator.

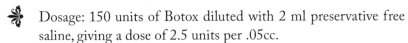 Self dilation: Patients and their partners spend the next two days practicing with insertion and removal of the various sized dilators. This is done with guidance from our staff. Patients also are instructed to sleep with the medium sized #4 dilator for the first two or three nights, then alternate nights after that.

* Note: Two months after her procedure, Maria continued to persist with dilation, though the process took effort, given the severity of her vaginismus and her decade-long history with this condition. She wrote to me, "I FINALLY got #5 in last night and slept with it for about three hours...seems like it's taken me FOREVER! But I'm glad that I still continue to move in the right direction. It took quite some time, almost an hour in fact, to get it in, but I refused to give up and it worked."

Waking Up to a New You...
and Painless Penetration

In January 2009, I was walking with my wife, Janet, along the beach on Honeymoon Island off the west coast of Florida. We were discussing my treatment program for vaginismus, which I was continuing to develop and refine with each new patient. Granted, this may not have been the most likely topic of conversation for a place called Honeymoon Island. On the other hand, there was something fitting about the location, given that so many of my patients discovered their inability to consummate their marriages on their honeymoon nights.

At the time, the vaginismus patients who came to see me were being treated with Botox injections under anesthesia in our surgical center. After they had rested, they were sent home or to their hotel with a brand new, unopened box of six progressively larger dilators. About five or so days post-procedure, after the Botox had kicked in and alleviated the muscle spasms, these patients were instructed to start practicing with the smallest dilator in their kit, and then work their way up. The goal was to progress to the largest dilators; either the fifth one in size, Miss Pink, or the sixth and largest dilator in the box, aptly nicknamed Mr. Big Blue, given its six-inch stature.

Dilation, the act of making something wider or causing it to expand, has long been prescribed as a treatment for vaginismus. The process helps to gradually stretch the tight vaginal muscles, which is necessary in order to achieve comfortable intercourse. Many physicians, sex therapists, and online vaginismus communities promote relaxation exercises followed by dilation as one of the most effective ways for women to overcome vaginismus. For some women, dilation is indeed the solution they have been seeking. Yet, in other cases, particularly for women suffering from the highest levels of vaginismus, trying to overcome this disorder by attempting to relax while using dilators can make for very slow, painful progress, or no progress at all.

* *

During the procedure you are asleep, thank goodness, and when you wake up, you will have the dilator inside of your vagina, which is amazing in itself, especially if you have believed for so long that nothing could ever go in there. One of the bigger revelations to me was when the nurse had me take the dilator completely out for the first time. I mean, I knew what the dilators looked like, and I knew I had one inside of me (#5), but when I took it out for the first time and looked at it, I still could not believe that I had just pulled that big thing out of me!

* *

Most of the women I have seen for this condition fall into this second category. These are the patients who have purchased dilators, but they cannot even bring themselves to break the seal on the box. Alternatively, they manage to get so far as to insert the smallest dilator, but cannot advance to the next larger size, let alone come to terms with the idea of intercourse. These women often try for several weeks to dilate according to the instructions provided in the kit, but, ultimately, the fear of penetration and pain prove too difficult to overcome. And so they are confronted with what feels like another failure.

In my own treatment program for vaginismus, we emphasize the critical importance of dilation. With my early patients, however, I discovered that even after they were treated with Botox, the process of working with the dilators still remained stressful and time-consuming. Most of these women would take between one to three hours to insert a medium dilator, and some of them needed three months or longer to work their way up to the larger sizes and transition to intercourse. In most of these cases, it wasn't the now minor pain and burning, which is common when you initially stretch any tight muscle, that intimidated them, but the fact that they still had to deal with the idea of penetration, which often remained a serious mental block.

I had two perspectives about these cases. On the one hand, over 90 percent of my vaginismus patients persisted and achieved pain-free intercourse within three months, a relatively short time considering the condition had gripped them for years, or even decades, in some instances. On the other hand, it seemed to me that most of my patients still had to work too hard at dilation. Given the Botox injections, I felt they should be able to progress faster and with more confidence…but how?

A Seaside Epiphany

My wife, Janet, was aware of the amount of time my office was spending communicating with our patients, often coaxing them through their fears as they labored through the process of progressive dilation. She offered this suggestion as we walked on the beach: "If dilation is so important in treating vaginismus, why don't you just insert a dilator when the patient is under anesthesia for the Botox injections? That way, when they wake up in the recovery room, they'll know a dilator is already in place."

Talk about an epiphany! I immediately recognized the potential in Janet's suggestion. Soon after this conversation, I realized that I could also coat the indwelling dilator with a topical anesthetic to immediately numb the vagina, and then inject a long-acting anesthetic so that the patient would not feel the dilator inside them for about seven hours. With an indwelling dilator already in place after the Botox procedure, this could provide the psychological breakthrough these women needed to overcome their fear of penetration.

As it turns out, dilation under anesthesia also provided a jump start to the physiological process of actually stretching the tight muscles. It only takes muscles about thirty seconds to relax after inserting a speculum. These muscles also stay dilated after the larger dilators are introduced, while the patients are under anesthesia.

After Janet made her suggestion to insert the dilators while the patients were under anesthesia, my first scheduled patient was Kelsie, who had suffered with vaginismus for six and a half years. Kelsie, you may recall, was the patient who suggested that there should be a Level 5 on the Lamont scale, equating the times she attempted intercourse to "…an explosion of fear and nerves in your head. THE PAIN IS SO BAD!"

By the time Kelsie scheduled an appointment with me, her self esteem was shot and she reported that she had even told her husband at one point to divorce her or find a girlfriend because she felt there was no hope for her to have sex. Undeterred, her husband promised to help her keep looking for a cure. "There is something seriously wrong with your vagina," he told her. "I don't care what the doctors say. I know it's not all in your head."

* *

I'm no longer scared of inserting the dilators because I know how they feel inside of me.

* *

Kelsie came to me about eighteen months after having that conversation with her spouse, and I proposed the idea of inserting a dilator in her vagina while she was under anesthesia for the Botox injections. The idea would be to leave it in place even after she woke up from sedation. After talking it over, Kelsie agreed to be my "guinea pig," fully aware that I had not performed this procedure yet with other patients.

It is important to emphasize that women with vaginismus have perfectly normal, healthy vaginas. In fact, one of the main reasons I perform an internal examination before every Botox procedure is to determine this, as well as to confirm a diagnosis of vaginismus.

Women with vaginismus may believe their vagina is very small, or that they don't even have a "hole" as one of my patients thought, but in reality, there is nothing wrong with the anatomy of their vaginas. Once their muscle spasms are alleviated under anesthesia, dilation is no longer a physical challenge and there is no danger to the patient. In fact, a woman's vagina is naturally structured to accommodate a large dilator, penis, or, when fully dilated, even a baby's head.

In the operating room, Kelsie's internal examination revealed spasm in her entry muscle and mid vagina, even when she was under a medium level of sedation. This was exactly as she had described it to me—her vagina was "shut down," like a tight fist. Kelsie's muscles eventually relaxed as she fell into a deeper sleep, and I targeted the Botox injections to the affected areas. I then progressively dilated her, starting with the smallest dilator, and then easily working my way up to the #5 of six, which was left in her vagina post-procedure.

The recovery nurse, our surgical technician, Kelsie's husband who had been in the operating room with me, and I stood by Kelsie's bedside in the recovery room. She was a bit groggy, so it was necessary to wait with nervous excitement a few minutes before asking her if she remembered that we would be leaving a dilator in her vagina. Because of the numbing medication, Kelsie could not detect that the dilator was inside her until she reached down and felt it.

* *

I stayed in the recovery room for a couple of hours. I was encouraged to gently move the dilator out and push it back in. When I managed to do it once I was in shock that I was moving something in and out of me without freaking out.

* *

A few days later, Kelsie recorded her thoughts on a video diary she was producing about her experience with vaginismus. The following describes those first few hours in our recovery room, and how she felt after realizing a full-size dilator was inside her vagina:

"It was funny at first because Dr. Pacik and my husband and the staff, they were just waiting. They didn't know if I was going to wake up with a dilator inside me and just flip out. We had figured maybe waking up with something already inside me, and not feeling that horrible pain, would trigger something. And you know what? It did. I woke up and it was exactly what we had hoped. It flipped a switch in my head. I'm okay! Something is inside me and I'm okay! I'm not feeling pain. It's not blowing up in my head, and I'm not feeling like I'm going to die and I can't take it."

Kelsie goes on to describe her experience after she returned home: "It's now day four and my progress is monumental. I'm up to inserting dilator #5 on my own, the next to the last size. I would say the first two days I was still panicky, pretty scared, but by day three the panic attacks were gone, and now I have more hope than I did before. I'm so happy that I did this..."

Not quite two weeks later, Kelsie returns to her online diary: "I have great news. I was able to have intercourse day twelve. It actually happened! I felt relief and am so grateful that I wasn't the one person the Botox did not work on. I wouldn't say it was painful, but there was discomfort. It felt like a really strong burning and stretching sensation. Dr. Pacik said that was very normal. The muscles need to be stretched. That lasted less than five minutes."

Six weeks later Kelsie continues to record in her diary: "I want to say by the fifth time I had intercourse, I didn't even feel any of the burning anymore at all. Just a little bit of stretching. Just because my muscles haven't been used."

Kelsie goes on to talk about her emotional reaction to intercourse. "…the pit in the stomach, the fear I can't do it, I guess all that had been from just attempting to have intercourse before. The panic and dread and feeling nauseous—it was gone. It was like I was a new person."

While Kelsie was able to have sex within two weeks after her procedure, she still wanted to wait until all the effects of the Botox had worn off before calling herself completely "cured." Approximately eleven months after the procedure she recorded the following on her video diary, "Yesterday, January 31, I was so happy because I was cured! There was no burning. It was just like normal. This is what normal sex is like! I'd always hoped for the day that I'd be the aggressor: 'You know what, honey, we're getting busy tonight.' Last night my husband said, 'I'm getting tired,' and I'm like, 'You need to fulfill your husbandly duties.'"

On the video, Kelsie's smile is a mile wide. (Note: To view Kelsie's video diary: visit www.youtube.com/bravewomenspeak)

The Janet Technique

The use of an indwelling dilator inserted under anesthesia is now a key component in my treatment program. The patients are easily able to rotate, remove, and replace the dilator after waking up in the recovery room because the vagina is numb after the procedure, thanks to the combination of an injected long-acting anesthetic and a topical anesthetic.

After the patient has become comfortable with the idea of touching and turning the dilator (remember, for some of these women, this is the first time they have had any contact with their vaginas), they then practice removing and re-inserting the dilator—yet another milestone! To confirm that the patient has reached an adequate comfort level with dilation, we ask them to return to our office for additional practice and instruction over the next couple days. This process is critical to set the stage for continued progress after the woman returns home. The patients are also encouraged to allow their partners to help insert and remove the dilators as much as possible, which furthers their mutual progress toward intercourse.

I consider the portion of our treatment program that involves dilation under anesthesia as the "Janet technique" in honor of my wife. I bless her for having this insight, which has made such a difference for my patients. The immediate change in these women when they realize they can have pain-free penetration is profound. I saw it with Kelsie, our first patient who woke up with a dilator in place, and recently saw it with one of our newest patients, Wendy, who has suffered from vaginismus for twenty-two years. Wendy could not even look at the dilators before her treatment without feeling faint, but she was able to easily remove and re-insert the largest dilator within the hour after her procedure.

The battle to overcome vaginismus may not be completely won when patients wake up in the recovery room with a dilator in place, but it is a triumph that automatically reduces the severity of their vaginismus from a Lamont Level 4 or 5 to a Level 2.

For a woman who has never experienced any form of penetration, not even tampons, this marks a significant emotional breakthrough, and begins the important physical process of stretching the vagina, which has been in a tightened, spastic state, sometimes for years. To realize that penetration is possible and painless, to know that her vagina is healthy and normal and, at that very moment, is accommodating a dilator even larger than the size of an average penis—this new awareness for a vaginismus patient may be even more responsible than Botox for breaking the cycle of fear and pain associated with this condition.

Step by Step: Dilation under Anesthesia and in the Recovery Room

* *

❧ In the operating room, patients are examined under anesthesia to confirm a "normal" vagina in length, width and compliance—the ability to stretch, enough for a baby's head to pass through during childbirth.

❧ Once sedated so that the patient experiences no pain, and the vaginal muscles no longer contract upon contact, patients are injected with Botox.

❧ After receiving the Botox injections, patients are progressively dilated, with most of them easily able to accommodate the largest of the six dilators. The dilator is left in the vagina post-procedure.

❧ In the recovery room, patients often experience an emotional breakthrough as they realize that they are experiencing pain-free penetration, an achievement most of them had previously believed impossible. This large dilator remains in the vagina for about one hour.

❧ Over the next three to four hours, patients are supported and advised as they practice with the dilators in the recovery room, first rotating the dilators, then moving them slowly in and out of the vagina.

❧ Patients are also taught proper hygiene for simple cleaning of the dilators. (Note: toxic shock is not a problem because the dilators are not porous.)

❧ Patients return home or to their hotel with a dilator in place. Tight panties or biking shorts help keep the dilator in place as they walk around. They are instructed to sleep with the dilator size that is comfortable, usually #4. Keeping the dilator in place overnight has proven to be another key to success!

❧ The next morning, dilation continues in the office. Most patients arrive concerned about this process because the local anesthesia has worn off by now. This is why sleeping with the dilator is so important, because it assures that the muscles are already well dilated. Typically, dilation back up to the largest dilator is something most patients are able to achieve in a short period of time, even without the benefit of the local anesthetic. This instills further confidence that they are on the road to recovery.

❧ Over the next two or three days, patients continue working with the dilators in our recovery room. In this way, they continue to get comfortable with the process of dilation even before the Botox has had a chance to take effect. Patients also receive counseling related to intercourse and a healthy sex life.

❧ We often treat two or three vaginismus patients on the same day at our practice. With their approval, we facilitate group discussions among them and encourage them to stay in touch after returning home. For many patients, this is the first time they have discussed their condition with other women.

❧ Within two or three days, the change in most patients is notable. They no longer present as meek or scared, or see themselves as self-described "freaks." Instead, they appear much more control and determined to succeed. My staff can see these changes, as can the women themselves.

Practice Makes Perfect:
Miss Pink, Mr. Big Blue, and Beyond

Congratulations. The internal examination that was performed under anesthesia confirmed you have a perfectly healthy and normal-sized vagina. You have come through your thirty-minute Botox procedure with flying colors. In a matter of days, the Botox will take effect, and the involuntary muscle spasms that made sex virtually impossible will no longer be an issue.

You also have achieved another significant breakthrough. You now know that you can achieve vaginal penetration because you have already experienced it, first under anesthesia with an indwelling dilator, then in our recovery room as you practiced inserting and removing different size dilators. This occurred even before the Botox took effect.

So, are you cured? Are you ready for intercourse?

Almost. The Botox treatment and your early success with dilation are huge steps forward—addressing the physical barrier to penetration and significantly disrupting the cycle of pain and fear associated with it. However, it is critical you remain committed to dilating on a regular basis in the coming days and weeks. This will reinforce your emotional comfort level with penetration, and it will better prepare your vaginal muscles for your first experiences with intercourse.

Post Botox: Using the Dilators to Stretch and De-Stress

Consider dilation as a "warm-up" to intercourse, the same way you would want to warm up or stretch your muscles before exercise. The inside of a vagina is naturally designed to accommodate an average-size dilator or penis. For women with vaginismus, the vagina has been tightly locked, sometimes for many years. That is why progressive dilation is critical. It works to gently and gradually loosen up those clenched, spastic vaginal muscles. When you transition from dilators to intercourse, you feel much more ready, both physically and emotionally. .

Over the course of three days or so after a patient's procedure, the patient and her partner, if applicable, receive considerable counseling on dilation, allowing them ample time to get used to working with the dilators in the comfort of our recovery room. After the Botox treatment, the patient should begin a routine of dilating twice every day for one to two hours at a stretch, always coating the dilator with lots of lubricant. Starting with a lubricant that includes a topical anesthetic will make the process easier. Later, when you feel ready, you can switch to a regular lube. Each time you dilate you should find it easier and easier to advance through to the larger sizes.

* *

Everything is going fine, although I have one complaint about dilating—I can't laugh when a dilator is in! It hurts. Maybe that will go away as the muscles relax. Also, we did try to play "just the tip." I am not sure how far we actually got, but I think we got the tip in...or at least knocking. :)

* *

The incorporation of Kegel pelvic floor contractions often makes inserting the dilators easier. Patients are instructed to perform a series of five to ten strong Kegel exercises, holding each contraction for a few seconds. On the last contraction, the patient should squeeze hard and completely release the pelvic floor while applying pressure to the dilator. Some resistance is usually encountered, and patients often need to apply additional pressure to get past the entry muscle. Once the dilator slips through this area, however, the rest is relatively easy. (Note: Even women without vaginismus sometimes experience resistance at the entry point to the vagina.)

This is where persistence is important, as the tip of the dilator needs to pass through the initial area of resistance to allow it to be fully inserted. Because most patients have spasm of the entry muscle only, once the dilator passes this muscle the remaining insertion offers less resistance. When you are ready to advance to intercourse a similar technique can be used. Think of how the penis is shaped like a dilator, narrower at the tip and thicker in the body.

In addition to practicing dilation during the day, you will also want to sleep with the medium #4 dilator in place every other night. In fact, some patients find it completely comfortable to sleep with the medium dilator nightly for the first two weeks. The #5 dilator is a little too big for sleeping comfort for most women. This overnight stretch of dilation can make a big difference in terms of speeding up your readiness for intercourse.

Once the Botox begins working, about two to five days post procedure, moving up to the larger dilators usually becomes easier. After about two weeks of working with the dilators daily and sleeping with the medium #4 in place every other night, most patients are comfortable inserting Miss Pink and Mr. Big Blue. For some women, an inch or two of the pink or blue dilator may protrude beyond the vaginal entrance, depending on the length of the vagina. Once you are consistently dilating with Miss Pink or Mr. Big Blue, you are ready to try intercourse!

To make the transition from dilators to intercourse as comfortable as possible, it is helpful to dilate with one of these larger-sized dilators for approximately fifteen to thirty minutes immediately before intercourse. In fact, some women find that intercourse is easier than inserting Mr. Big Blue, given that even an erect penis is softer and more yielding than a dilator. You will want to continue your schedule of dilation for several more months, or even up to a year after you have started having intercourse, to continue to actively stretch your vagina in a way that isn't possible through intercourse alone.

The time it takes to transition from dilators to intercourse can be as short as a few days to a couple of months. For some patients, the process may be more slow-going, but that, too, is okay. Every woman we treat has already experienced success with the #5 or #6 dilator while in our recovery room, but some remain fearful of practicing with Mr. Big Blue, or even Miss Pink, on their own. This has been described to me in these terms: The hand guiding the dilator feels "paralyzed" and does not want to cooperate.

This reluctance is understandable, given the woman's history of vaginismus. As one patient shared, "It did take me a little time to get used to inserting the dilator on my own, but I just had to continue reminding myself that I had inserted the dilator before. Prior to the procedure, I had NEVER been able to give myself such positive talk, but now I knew I could do it again."

Often patients who continue to struggle those first few weeks or months with the lingering fear of penetration assume that they will be the exception to the rule, that they won't be "cured" of vaginismus, despite the Botox treatment. As explained by the patient quoted in the previous paragraph, however, it may take hours at first to insert a dilator, despite the fact that vaginal spasms are no longer an issue.

It is also normal to have a sore spot due to the trauma of repeated dilation, and even some setbacks with dilation. If this occurs, simply take a break for a day or two and then resume, always with a smaller dilator, inserting it in such a way as to avoid the sore spot. Gradually, you can move up again in size. Even dilating for ten or fifteen minutes with a smaller dilator is still worthwhile.

This also holds true during menstruation. Keep dilating if possible, for shorter periods if necessary. If you do stop dilating because of heavy flow, then resume as soon as possible, starting with the medium dilators and working your way back up to the larger sizes. This is also a good time to try using a tampon, which is similar to inserting a small dilator. This, too, marks progress toward penetration, given that most women with vaginismus have never used a tampon.

The bottom line: for some women the dilation process and overcoming vaginismus is a marathon, not a sprint. It is important to pace yourself, and not feel discouraged if you are unable to have intercourse within weeks after the procedure. With persistence and patience, even our patients who struggled with dilation in those first few weeks or months were able to progress to Miss Pink or Mr. Big Blue on their own…and you can, too.

The Fine Art of Dilation: Q & A

Q: Do I do the Kegel exercises with the dilator in or out?
A: Do the Kegels before you insert the first dilator, and then repeat them with the dilator in place before advancing to the next larger size. By fatiguing and relaxing the pelvic floor it will be easier to insert progressively larger dilators.

Q: You said I need to be dilating at least twice a day. Is that better than dilating once for a very long time?
A: Yes. The more periods of time spent with dilation, the more rapid the progress. However, for patients who do not have time in the morning or during the day, dilating for two hours in the evening does seem to work quite well.

Q: You recommend dilating all night every other night. Is there any point in sleeping with the dilator every night? Will this help or hurt my progress?
A: My very motivated patients sleep with the medium dilator every night for several weeks. The medium dilator, #4 of six, seems to be well tolerated. If irritation develops, you can use smaller dilators or skip some of the evenings to allow things to settle down. Ibuprofen or Tylenol can help for control of discomfort.

Q: In one week my period will start. Can I stop using the dilators until it's over?
A: If your flow is too heavy, it's okay to skip a couple days, although it would be better to continue some dilation while having your menses, even if it is just ten or fifteen minutes at a time. You may prefer during this interlude to dilate in the tub. Once you succeed with the larger dilators, try using a tampon. Most vaginismus patients have never been able to accomplish this, and, this too, will represent a breakthrough. When your period is over, start again with the medium dilator for a day or

two, and then advance to #5 and #6 when comfortable. Slow dilation does make the entire process easier for some women, and you will still accomplish your goals.

Q: I am still bleeding slightly from the Botox injections. Is that normal?
A: A small amount of blood is of no concern. There may be residual blood in the vagina from the injections. Use lots of lube and introduce the dilators slowly.

Q: Am I supposed to walk around and do activities while dilating, or should I relax and be still?
A: The exact specifics about dilating are unimportant. What matters is that you dilate twice a day for about an hour each time, and you sleep with the medium-sized dilator every other night. Whether you relax or are active while dilating depends on your comfort level, but you do need to advance to the larger dilators.

Q: Is there any method to help my buttocks and thigh muscles relax while dilating?
A: Bending over two pillows in the face-down position relaxes the pelvic floor muscles. Some women find this comfortable and use this position for their early attempts at intercourse, as well. Lying flat on a bed, face up, your head on a pillow or two, with your legs up and knees flexed (the "missionary" position) can also be relaxing. Measured breathing and relaxing your mind is also helpful.

Q: When I dilate and then have intercourse, I still sometimes feel a "burning." Is this normal?
A: Any burning that you feel is related to stretching. Stretched muscles tend to burn. As you continue progressing with the dilators this will disappear, usually within a few weeks. Some sex therapists recommend using dilators for one year after treatment, even after you have progressed to intercourse.

Q: I still need around four minutes to insert the medium or pink dilator. Will this be a problem for intercourse, that I can't insert the dilators faster?

A: No. Even women without vaginismus need time to prepare for penetration. That is why most men intuitively know to stimulate women with their fingers before intercourse, to help get them lubricated and stretch the vagina. This is also why it is best for the man to insert the penis slowly and gradually, to avoid a painful experience for the woman.

Q: My partner can only insert the tip of his penis when we try intercourse. What is wrong?

A: It's just fine, even recommended, to start with minimal penetration intercourse. Continued fear of penile penetration is difficult to overcome, but by your partner starting slowly without thrusting, you will be able to relax and advance. If you continue slowly you will achieve full penetration with time.

Q: I had sex on Sunday, six days after my procedure! I am very happy! Do I still need to dilate if I have had intercourse?

A: Intercourse is not a substitute for continued dilation. The reason is because your partner cannot sustain an erection for the length of time needed to help continue to stretch your vagina. Therefore, you still need to use the dilators, even if you have already advanced to intercourse, for about three or four months, or even up to a year. That said, some women get enough benefit by just dilating for fifteen minutes a day once they are comfortable with intercourse. If burning resumes, increase the dilation schedule. Remember, burning is related to stretching of the muscles.

Q: I try to dilate every day for at least forty-five minutes. Now when my husband and I have intercourse, he says my vagina is over-dilated. Does this get better when the Botox wears off?

A: Dilation is helpful for you to achieve full, comfortable intercourse, so even if you are somewhat stretched from doing so, don't stop. You can try dilating less prior to intercourse, as long as you don't feel discomfort or burning. As the Botox wears off, the vaginal muscles will have more tone, and you will likely feel a difference with both intercourse and orgasm. In the meantime, you may want to hold your husband's penis tightly while he is inside you to help him climax.

Q: Will I get vaginismus again if I do not have sex?
A: You should have no recurrence of vaginismus if you continue to dilate on a regular basis, even in the absence of intercourse.

Q: Can I have the treatment if I don't have a partner?
A: Yes. You just need to maintain a dilation schedule until you meet someone and become comfortable with intercourse.

Q: I'm two years post treatment and am starting to feel a burning again. Does this mean that I am having a recurrence of vaginismus?
A: Sometimes if there is no sexual activity for weeks in a row, the vagina needs to go through the stretching process again. A burning sensation usually just means you need to get on an increased dilation schedule, and start sleeping with the medium dilator again. Once the muscles are adequately re-stretched, the burning should disappear. It's also a good idea to try having intercourse at least once a week. You may also sleep better!

Tips to Help with Dilation after the Botox Procedure

Set a Schedule for Success. Dilate at least twice a day for one to two hours at a time and advance to the larger dilators during this time. Moving to larger dilators can usually be done after dilating with smaller sizes for as little as fifteen or thirty minutes. Sleep with the medium dilator every other night. When you are comfortable dilating with the largest sizes, you are ready to have intercourse, but continue dilating even after you have moved on to intercourse, at least until all muscle "burning" is gone.

Use lubricants. Because Botox interferes with the parasympathetic nervous system let down, you will need lots of lube for the next four months, both when dilating and having intercourse. Lidocaine, a lubricant with a topical anesthetic, is safe to use in minimal amounts. At my practice, we use a 2 percent strength Lidocaine mixed with Surgilube on a regular basis with our vaginismus patients, although some patients require 5 percent strength, a dosage more often used by physical therapists for patients with pelvic floor pain issues. The Lidocaine may cause slight burning on application but this disappears after the numbness sets in.

Start by applying a dime-size amount to both the vaginal entrance and the dilator. The best approach is to massage the lubricant into the tissues of the opening area and just inside the vagina, and allow the numbing agent to work for several minutes prior to dilating. If you plan to progress to intercourse, your partner should wear a condom so that he does not become desensitized. The condom can be lubricated, as well.

I often advise couples to make the application of the Lidocaine jelly part of their foreplay. This gives it time to work, plus it makes applying it more fun. And always allow yourselves plenty of time for foreplay to help stimulate your arousal and desire. (Note: most of my patients have discontinued the use of Lidocaine by the time they are ready to try intercourse. At this point, you can experiment with any one of the lubes. Just be sure to use plenty!)

Breathe. As with advanced stretching techniques used in sports or physical therapy, timed breathing can also help enormously with dilation to increase relaxation and therefore ease of insertion. Try taking a few deep breaths from your stomach utilizing a technique called abdominal breathing. On about the third breath, as you inhale slowly, start sliding the dilator into the vagina. With each successive exhale, try to push the dilator in a bit further.

Do Kegels. Always start with a dilator that goes in easily, even if it is smaller. After the dilator has been inside your vagina for about fifteen minutes, do a series of Kegel exercises with breathing. To do a Kegel, take a deep breath, hold it, squeeze the pelvic floor for five or ten seconds, blow out the air and fully relax the pelvic floor. Repeat five times. At the last Kegel, with everything relaxed, insert the next size dilator. In this way you should be able to advance comfortably to the next bigger size. Don't give up!

Get Distracted. This advice came from one of my patients, who felt that concentrating too much on pushing in the dilator only made it more difficult. She had more success when she was distracted, either by the TV or her partner. She remarked, "In the early stages of using the smallest dilator I made sure my husband sat with me so we could have a chat. It completely took my mind away from what I was doing, and before I knew it the dilator had gone in."

Try All the Angles. When inserting a dilator, try different positions to see which one feels most comfortable. One of my patients could only insert the dilator in an upright position, for example. When lying down she felt she lost control. During intercourse, this translated to her being on top, which helped her get used to penile penetration.

Pause and Regroup. If you feel a sharp pain like you are hitting that wall again, do not push yourself to go further with the dilator, but do not pull it out either. Just hold the dilator in place until the pain dissipates. When you feel more comfortable, push and progress a little further. This kind of patience is worth it. Soon, the process won't take so long, but for now it is important to persist.

Don't Forget your Lover. It's easy to get into your own routine with dilation, but sooner rather than later it's a good idea to involve your partner in the process. Have your partner insert your dilator, or use it as a toy for stimulation. This allows him to feel comfortable with the process, the vagina, and the angle the penis will have to be inserted. The man's participation also takes the challenge of vaginismus out of the realm of "the woman's problem" and makes it an issue to resolve together.

Be patient. At first, it may take an hour or more to insert a dilator, but persist. Generally, the entry muscle is the most stubborn barrier to get past, but with patience, you can relax into it. Remember, the Botox is working so you won't hit that wall! And while it may feel weird or uncomfortable to have a big dilator inside you, it won't be painful.

Enjoy a warm bath. What a difference soaking in a hot tub can make in terms of helping you unwind and make dilation not only easier, but even arousing with practice.

Wash the dilators. Wash each dilator with soap and water after every use. Because the dilators are not porous, there is no danger of toxic shock syndrome.

Set an Outside Goal of Four Months. The muscle-relaxing effects of Botox last about four months, so ideally you will want to complete your transition from dilators to intercourse within that time frame. Most of my patients are able to have intercourse within a few weeks, but don't give up and don't worry if you need more time. Remember that your partner's penis will likely be more comfortable than the largest dilators. As a patient once said, "You were right about the real thing being easier than the big blue one."

At Long Last Love:
Achieving Intimacy

INCHING TOWARD INTERCOURSE

It is recommended that patients start with minimal penetration the first few times they attempt intercourse after the Botox procedure. As the phrase "minimal penetration" implies, the man should insert just the tip of the penis into the vagina. Similar to practicing with the dilator, the penis should be inserted slowly to gradually stretch the entry muscle. The man should then refrain from any thrusting or movement once the penis is inside the vagina. This process will help the woman feel more in control, and it also gives her time to communicate her level of comfort every step of the way.

Obviously, minimal penetration requires a modicum of trust between partners. The woman has to feel assured her partner will not advance more quickly than she can tolerate. The process of building trust will pay off not only as you progress toward full intercourse, but also after you become fully comfortable in your sexual relationship and explore other avenues of arousal and pleasure.

Most women report some discomfort and/or vaginal burning when they first have intercourse, even after dilating for a few weeks. This discomfort is nothing like the excruciating pain associated with vaginismus, but rather the natural response to stretching a tight muscle. You might think of it as the difference between pain and mild discomfort. Regardless, the longer and more frequently you dilate, the sooner the discomfort abates. It should then completely disappear, likely within a month or so after you start having intercourse.

It is also recommended that patients purchase a vibrator or dildo such as "Mr. SoReal," which is about as large as the average penis and looks and feels more "real" than a dilator, hence the name. Using this kind of sex toy can be beneficial during the transition to intercourse because its size and similarity to a real penis will help alleviate the initial stretching pain more quickly.

Will sex be terrific once you achieve the momentous milestone of penile penetration? Can you expect bells and whistles and an orgasm, to boot? No, not at first. It may take several months before you start experiencing pleasure and have your first orgasm—and even then, that orgasm may have more to do with forms of sexual stimulation other than intercourse.

What is more, Botox changes the way the muscles react. It doesn't cause numbness, but it does reduce muscle activity. Some women, and men as well, report intercourse feels almost "mechanical" rather than spontaneous those first times with their partners.

These reactions are common, and no cause for discouragement. As your body and mind continue to adjust to intercourse, and as you and your partner become more sexually active and aware of each other's personal erotic zones, you have every reason to expect intercourse to evolve into true intimacy. Just remember to go slow at first, and inch by inch you'll eventually advance from painless intercourse to pleasurable sex.

Feels Like the First Time: First-Person Accounts

Every day our office receives several personal e-mails from patients we have treated. Our patients write to provide progress reports, ask questions, or just say thanks. These updates are particularly gratifying when I recall the pre-procedure questionnaires completed by these women, often reflecting their frustration, and even desperation, to find a treatment for their vaginismus. When these women describe how they have finally achieved intercourse after so many years of struggle, pain, and fear, their success reinforces what the practice of medicine is all about for me and my staff. This feedback also helps me hone my treatment protocols.

The following e-mail communications from four former patients represent experiences that are common to many of our vaginismus

Twelve Days Post Botox Procedure

He: "I'm disappointed she didn't have an orgasm."

She: "I'm just in awe that it wasn't hurting. So orgasm was the last thing on my mind."

patients during the first weeks and months following treatment. While every patient is unique and progresses at her own pace, I believe sharing these first-person accounts, preceded by a brief introduction of each woman's personal history, offers a deeper understanding of the "average" journey, with all its ups and downs, of overcoming vaginismus and inching your way to intercourse.

Frances

Patient overview: Frances, 24, was accompanied by her mother when she came to our office for treatment. Frances had a five-year history of severe pain with pelvic examinations and intercourse. She first noticed that something was wrong when trying to use tampons at age fifteen. Each time she tried to have intercourse since age nineteen she, like so many, described it as "like hitting a wall." A doctor recommended surgery (a vestibulectomy) but she declined. She spent years treating the condition with drugs, counseling, and physical therapy, all of which failed. Diagnosis: Lamont Level 4 Primary Vaginismus.

From Frances, seven days after treatment:
I am continuing to use Big Blue. I still have a slight discomfort with insertion. I actually think it is the stretching I am feeling but it is gone after a minute or so. I experience normal pressure on my bladder with the dilator in, but I am not having any urethral irritation. I am still a little sensitive around my urethra but it seems to be lessening every day. I am not having any urgency issues.

I still am able to do Kegels. When I tense up (despite my best efforts not to!) with the dilator inside me, I do not feel the immense pain or discomfort I have felt in the past. So I am assuming the muscle spasm is much less at this point. I think moving the dilators in and out without pain is the most important step at this point. I could never do this before. I could never have them in for thirty minutes without pain. I am happy with how things are going so far. I think I am still partly in shock that I have made so much progress in such a short amount of time.

From Frances, ten days after treatment:
Last night we started with minimal penetration and there was no pain. We decided to continue into normal intercourse. I was on top. Although this position allows me to be in control, I think it made for deeper penetration than maybe we needed the first time around.

The initial pain is one hundred percent better and gone. There was some discomfort. I can't quite pinpoint if it was just normal discomfort from not using my vagina functionally for the past five years, or still some "trigger points." However, I did have some observations. There was penetration for ten minutes and I am thinking it was just a little too much for the first try. I think we both were quite nervous, as well. We really didn't know what to expect.

This weekend we are going to try the position you described with the pillows under my stomach. We also didn't use the Lidocaine topical anesthetic which we will use this weekend. I was trying to be a tad spontaneous in hopes it wouldn't be so mechanical, but I think we need a little more planning next time. We are still very positive and hopeful. We will just have to work more at it.

From Frances, twelve days after treatment:
My husband and I had sex on both Saturday and Sunday. There was initial discomfort again but it left after about a minute or two. We used the Lidocaine/surgical lubricant. We also have been using the position where I'm on my stomach. Other than the initial discomfort there wasn't any other discomfort. Both times were less mechanical and more natural. I also do not have the immense soreness that I used to have after attempted intercourse. We are so happy to be at this point! We know there is still a lot of work ahead and that things will continue to get better."

From Frances, updates covering days twenty-four to thirty-two:
The most comfortable positions so far have been the stomach position and when we both are on our sides. These positions tend to lend to not such a deep penetration, which is good right now. I think me on top, although good for control, allows for more penetration. The standard missionary position isn't too bad but seems to be better if I have a pillow or two under my butt. This position was suggested to me by my physical therapist because she said it also causes the pelvic floor to be relaxed.

Sulekha

Patient Overview: Sulekha, 25, reported that she was brought up in a conservative Indian household, and was sexually abused, mainly touching and kissing, by a family member when she was a teenager. Married for five years, she had never been able to have intercourse or an examination. She only learned about vaginismus a year ago. Before her diagnosis, she went through a severe state of depression during the first three years of her marriage. She rated herself a ten, with sweating, nausea, fainting, on a scale of one to ten for degree of discomfort with vaginal penetration. She had purchased dilators, but had no luck using them due to her extreme fear. Sulekha came from New Zealand for treatment. Diagnosis: Level 5 Primary Vaginismus.

From Sulekha:
With Big Blue inside me, I wanted to take the dilator out only when my husband was ready to insert his penis. He was very uncomfortable with me using the dilator. It affected him so much psychologically that he had trouble even getting an erection, which is very abnormal for him. So we said we'll try again tomorrow.

Exactly a month after my Botox treatment, we faced the same problem. On top of it, while I was taking out the blue dilator from inside me, without realizing it, I pissed on my bedroom carpet. It was very frustrating for me emotionally. I went into depression and my husband promised that we'd try again the next day. I got my period the next day!

My husband read that it is common for the partners of vaginismus-suffering women to have erection issues. We decided to see our general practitioner to get a prescription of Viagra for him. He was really freaked out about the whole process but with courage he took the pill. I dilated for that hour waiting for the Viagra to work. When it finally worked, he fainted! It was an overdose for him (100 mg). He was sweating frantically and I was in a state of panic. He slept for almost four hours after that.

I spoke to my doctor about what happened. She told him to go for 50 mg. It took him a few days to get over his fear. It was two months and 16 days after my procedure when he took the 50 mg pill. But this time, when everything seemed to be working in our favor, my fears rose. Even though I had been dilating with ease, the idea of intercourse was completely different.

Initially, I was shutting my thighs on him but with the help of some mind talk, I convinced myself to go through this. Viagra really did help, as my husband could sustain his erection and it gave us more time to practice. He really did make me comfortable this time. Intercourse didn't come easy though. It was like teamwork. Even after the Botox, I could feel my muscles fighting back. So when he finally managed to get his tip in, I asked him to hold it there. I took some time to relax and then asked him to push again. This way, he would come in slowly at my pace rather than forcing himself in.

When he was completely inside me, it was so weird yet amazing! I couldn't feel him much. We both weren't sure whether he was inside me so I asked him to come out. Only when he came out, we realized that we had done it. So we tried again. This time it was a little quicker than the last time and we both took time to get used to the sensation. And then we tried again. And this time, I even allowed him small movements. I didn't feel any pain or pleasure. It does feel like my biggest achievement to date though.

Bridget

Patient Overview: Bridget first tried and failed to have intercourse on her honeymoon. She had been married two years when she came to see me for treatment of her vaginismus. She flew in from England with her husband. Bridget had heard many stories about how first-time sex involved pain and bleeding. She was never able to have an internal examination due to feelings of panic, and was often advised to relax and use lubricants to achieve intercourse. She also underwent a hymenectomy, which failed to address her symptoms of pain and fear. After the hymenectomy, she was still unable to insert even a small tampon. Diagnosis: Level 4 Primary Vaginismus.

From Bridget, twelve days post procedure:

You have probably guessed what the good news is!? Yes, we attempted last night and it happened!!! It was a bit uncomfortable and a little painful for me but nothing unbearable. It easily went in, as I had left the dilator in for 45 minutes before we tried. We were so happy and could not believe it. I thought I was dreaming!

My husband did use a condom but I found that very uncomfortable while trying so we tried without and it went in. He didn't ejaculate inside me though. Do you think that is okay or should we use condoms?

We are so happy! I still cannot believe it! I have also started my period today. I'm glad we did it before I started. Thank you so much.

From Bridget, twenty-one days post procedure:

Vaginismus should be a word that everyone is familiar with, from medical professionals to the general public. Because the term "vaginismus" is not part of people's daily vocabulary, when a woman develops this condition, she is baffled as to what and why this is happening to her. Just like there are leaflets on cancer, diabetes, etc. in clinics and hospitals, I think there should be leaflets or posters about vaginismus so that the information is there and available.

I remember my appointments with doctors/gynecologists. They were so horrible. I would start trembling and my body would become so defensive when their hands started to move towards me.

Now, it's a different story. I look back and think WHAT WAS ALL THE FUSS ABOUT? I can't believe I think that now. It's shocking that the idea of anything entering me or penetration does not scare me in the slightest now. I can't believe I suffered from vaginismus!

We are just so happy that this nightmare has come to an end! I feel cured. I don't have any fear of penetration any more. Even though intercourse is not completely pain-free and comfortable, I'm sure that will come with time. My husband is doing really well. He is extremely happy with our progress and we are just moving towards our future together, taking each day as it comes. We are so delighted and overjoyed!

Postscript:

At the time of this writing, Bridget is enjoying a healthy pregnancy.

Tracy

Patient Overview: Tracy, 29, was married for three years but unable to have intercourse because of severe pain. She consulted with five gynecologists who failed to diagnose vaginismus. One doctor prescribed Ativan, an anti-anxiety drug. She discovered and researched vaginismus online and tried to treat it with dilators as recommended on the site, but failed. At the time of treatment she reported her husband was afraid to touch her sexually and had been "talking" to other women online. "I love him and wonder if this huge nightmare would not have happened if I would have been able to make love to him." Diagnosis: Level 4 Primary Vaginismus.

From Tracy, one month post procedure:
I would like to give you the great news that we've finally been able to make love. THANK YOU! THANK YOU! There was no pain. I only felt a little bit of pressure but nothing major. The day we made love I didn't even have time to dilate at all. It just happened out of the blue. I was very scared because I knew I was not prepared. However, my husband said it was okay if I couldn't, but wanted us to try slowly and it worked. We have a lot to learn about each other's sexuality and we know it will take time and effort. But this is the answer we had been looking for over the past three years!

Inching toward Intercourse: Step by Step

❧ Dilate for fifteen to thirty minutes each time before intercourse. Let your partner occasionally insert the dilators for you so he can be part of the process and you can build trust. Guide him so he can help you feel comfortable. Remember to use lots of lubricant when you dilate and have intercourse, particularly because Botox can cause vaginal dryness. Later the dilator can be used as a sex toy to provide clitoral stimulation and arousal.

❧ For the first two or three tries at intercourse, only the tip of the penis should be inserted in the vagina. When this is comfortable, advance to just midway for two or three more times to continue the slow stretching of the vaginal muscles. This gradual process of penetration also helps continue to alleviate any fear.

❧ Once you are comfortable with minimal penetration, move towards three-quarters penetration for a few more times. This will give you another one to three weeks of partial penetration, and time to continue to overcome any discomfort or burning as the muscles stretch, or lingering fear. It will likely take time for intercourse to feel enjoyable, but you can expect sex to be more pleasurable as you continue to practice and learn about your own body and sexuality.

❧ Once your partner's penis is inside your vagina, have your partner just linger there without moving. This will allow you to have a slow stretch and the experience will be more comfortable for you. If you are on top, you may be better able to control the amount of movement and penetration.

✿ In between intercourse, continue your daily dilation schedule for thirty to sixty minutes at a time. (Note: dilation is actually more important than intercourse for proper stretching of the vagina.)

✿ If full penetration is too much even after trying these suggestions, simply continue minimal penetration until you feel ready. You will progress. It is just a matter of time.

✿ If you find it necessary to use a lubricant with a topical anesthetic, have your partner wear a condom. The local anesthesia on his skin may delay ejaculation.

✿ Consider using a vibrating dildo or an inflatable vibrator after dilation and before intercourse. This device should be slightly larger than your partner's penis, and is very effective for some women to become more comfortable with intercourse.

✿ It usually takes about a month to advance from the early use of dilators to full intercourse, so allow yourself enough time for this transition. That said, every woman is different. Do not feel rushed. Progress at your own pace, but do persist. It is worth it!

✿ Last, but hardly least, remember that Botox injections and dilation can help with the physical problem of vaginismus, but emotional issues related to penetration may linger even after the physical barriers to intercourse are removed. At this point, a good therapist can prove invaluable in helping you and your partner address any personal issues standing in the way of success. In addition, working with a certified sex therapist can help you tackle relationship problems and any unresolved resentment or anger, a common by-product among couples who have lived with the confusion and challenges of vaginismus.

Beyond Botox:
Complementary Therapies

L et's face it, a dilator is not a penis. So while you may have worked hard to overcome the physical barriers to penetration, you may still be ambivalent, or even downright scared, about having actual intercourse with a living, heavily breathing(!) partner. This is completely understandable given that dilation is a controlled situation, whereas intercourse and foreplay may make you feel less in control. Your experience with vaginismus and/or the causes behind it may also have led to you developing a sense of dread about sex. Accordingly, reframing your perception of intercourse as enjoyable may not happen automatically.

For women and couples who find the transition to intercourse challenging, there are a variety of complementary therapies that can help to enable a smoother journey from pain to pleasure.

Physical therapy and exercises focusing on the pelvic floor muscles, for example, can help vaginismus sufferers achieve a greater comfort level with dilation and penetration. In addition, psychotherapy, and specifically sex therapy, may be warranted to address personal or relationship issues that interfere with intimacy, issues that may have come to the fore once the "distraction" of vaginismus has been removed. Yet another, more experimental tool is a practice called Emotional Freedom Technique that uses tapping on acupuncture "meridian" points, speaking and breathing to address and "release" the initial traumatic feelings that caused vaginismus. Each of these therapies can assist in overcoming the conditioned response that sex means pain.

In the course of treating vaginismus patients, I have been fortunate to consult and collaborate with several therapists in these disciplines. The use of a team approach can make a significant difference for patients seeking to obtain a full recovery and satisfying love life.

Physical Therapy: The Final Stretch

According to physical therapist and certified sexual counselor Talli Rosenbaum, MSc, PT, who practices in Tel Aviv, Israel, physical therapy incorporates a number of techniques to help women overcome issues related to vaginismus. The physical therapist may provide anatomical information to the patient, such as teaching her about the vulva. The therapist may also provide home exercises to assist with desensitization, such as having the patient use a mirror to find the vaginal opening, and then touching and even inserting a finger inside the vagina.

Physical therapy also employs hands-on techniques, including manual therapy to help the vulvo-vaginal area become more flexible and ready to accept penetration. Another useful technique is pelvic floor biofeedback, in which a sensor placed in the vagina reads the muscle activity of the pelvic floor and displays it on a computer screen. The patient is then able to use this feedback to help her relax, as well as to strengthen and control her vaginal muscles in order to facilitate easier penetration.

For some patients with vaginismus, physical therapy alone, or in conjunction with psychotherapy, enables them to achieve comfortable intercourse over time. A colleague of mine in Manchester, New Hampshire, Erika Villemure, MPT, specializes in pelvic floor disorders and has successfully treated many vaginismus patients.

A woman with more severe levels of vaginismus, however, may be unable to progress with physical therapy, partly because the therapist may be unable to apply even the gentlest of therapeutic techniques before the patient retreats in fear or pain. Nonetheless, when these same therapeutic methods are used post-Botox with dilation, even Level 4 vaginismus patients with a failed history of pelvic floor work have made major strides.

A case in point is a former patient who was treated by Erika Villemure after undergoing the Botox procedure. Amanda, 27, struggled to overcome her vaginismus for the first three years of her marriage. "It felt as though my skin was being broken," she explained. "It was difficult to get comfortable and some bleeding would occur." Amanda also could not tolerate tampons or a Pap smear or internal examination from her gynecologist.

During this ordeal, Amanda's doctor diagnosed her with dyspareunia (painful sex), and referred her to Erika for pelvic floor physical therapy. Amanda's treatment program consisted of continuous ultrasound to the pelvis, employing sound waves to improve tissue relaxation and local blood flow; soft tissue mobilization; myofascial release, a hands-on technique that involves applying gentle sustained pressure into the connective tissue; and stretching. All of these techniques are intended to reduce spasm as the muscles of the vagina are stretched. They also can help the patient get comfortable with penetration by another person. Despite these efforts, Amanda's electromyography (EMG) revealed that she was still unable to relax her pelvic floor.

After five visits, Amanda discontinued physical therapy for insurance reasons, but returned almost two years later, still unable to achieve intercourse. By now, this condition was putting a strain on her marriage. In situations like this, many vaginismus patients try to avoid engaging in any behavior that is likely to arouse their partner. I don't want to be a tease, they think, or he may lose control and inadvertently force activity that I cannot tolerate. In Amanda's case, her lack of intimacy with her husband was pushing her marriage to the breaking point.

In Amanda's second round of physical therapy, she did make slow progress, but when she tried to advance to the largest size dilator she experienced bleeding. It was at this setback that Erika referred Amanda to me for Botox treatments.

In her pre-procedure examination, I noted Amanda to have maximum 4+/4 spasm of the vaginal entry muscle, even after she was under anesthesia. In addition, there was some minimal spasm of the two higher vaginal muscles, the PC and puborectalis. No wonder physical therapy could only achieve a limited amount of progress!

Immediately after the Botox injections, I was able to dilate Amanda to the largest dilator, which remained in place when she returned to the recovery room. After she was discharged, Amanda faithfully followed the comprehensive treatment program described in chapter 7, which includes ongoing dilation. Six days after receiving her Botox injections, she and her husband had intercourse with minimal, tolerable pain.

It was at this juncture, soon after Botox with dilation, that Amanda returned to her physical therapy program with Erika and made even further gains. With the Botox in effect, she benefitted significantly from manual stretching of her vagina, something that had been virtually impossible before her spasms had been alleviated. Her pelvic floor muscles showed normal tone, and she had no problem tolerating the insertion of a vaginal sensor.

Now, eight months post Botox, Amanda still sleeps with the medium dilator in place overnight, and dilates for about fifteen to thirty minutes before intercourse to avoid the possibility of any recurring physical or emotional discomfort. For patients such as Amanda, I recommend continuing a dilation routine for about a year. Amanda subsequently reported that she and her husband have been able to enjoy pain-free intercourse about once a week, and the marital tension brought on by vaginismus has all but disappeared.

"I was amazed at the change in her muscle structure and her overall comfort after undergoing her Botox treatment and using her dilators on a regular basis," said Erika. "Seeing Amanda from start to finish has been a very rewarding experience for me as a physical therapist."

Sex Therapy—Becoming Partners in Pleasure

For any couple, creating a mutually fulfilling, long-term love life takes ongoing communication and commitment. But for couples dealing with the legacy of vaginismus, developing a healthy sexuality may take some additional work, even after the pain factor is gone. Years of dealing with a confusing, undefined issue may have created a build-up of resentment and anger. It is so easy for couples to blame each other, and lose sight of the fact that the real problem is a physiological condition, not their partner.

So how do you move beyond the emotional baggage and negative patterns of the past? How do you communicate your sexual desires effectively? And what if you feel little or no desire for sex even after the issue of vaginismus has been resolved?

These are the kinds of questions sex therapy can help you address, particularly once you are free of the pain of vaginismus. In essence, sex therapy can provide an avenue for working on effective communication, emotional openness, trust, and mutual respect—all critical components in a healthy physical and emotional connection between partners.

But what exactly happens in sex therapy? Many people are intimidated by the notion, or have the false impression that sex therapy involves nudity or sexual contact between the therapist and the client. Rest assured, this is not the case. Basically, sex therapy is talk therapy in a safe controlled environment that offers each partner the opportunity to share feelings that they may have been too scared to say aloud to their partners, or even to themselves. Despite the fact that our sex drive is as normal as thirst or hunger, thoughts about sex and needs are often kept secret, even between partners.

• •

"Lots could be blamed on the vaginismus before. Now that this is no longer the issue, others came to light, in a very big way."
– Therapist for a post-Botox patient

• •

According to certified sex therapist Deborah Neel, PhD, co-author of *A Celebration of Sex Guidebook: A Couple's Guidebook to Passionate Intimacy,* sex therapy often starts with patient education, from how the human body works to the sexual response cycle for both males and females. Just one common misunderstanding: most couples wrongly assume there is a unisex model of sexual response, and that the woman is flawed in some way if she does not have the same hormonally driven desire as her male partner. The reality, however, is that although a couple may share the same sex drive during the first three to twenty-four months of the relationship, this is rarely maintained.

Another common misunderstanding among couples is that sexual fulfillment equates with orgasm. One reason for this confusion can be traced to the shifting definition of sexual desire. In the past, measurements of desire were oriented toward male characteristics: presence of sexual fantasies, erections or clitoral swelling, and an assertive biological need to be satisfied. More recently, however, the definition of sexual desire has included more female characteristics. For women, sexual desire is often seen as a willingness to be engaged sexually rather than a spontaneous craving for sex. Often, female desire tends to be motivated more by emotional connection or a longing for that connection. That is, emotional intimacy is more likely to lead to physical arousal.

For a woman who has struggled with vaginismus, sex therapy is one possible means of cultivating emotional intimacy with a partner. By working with a qualified therapist, she can help alleviate lingering feelings of isolation, embarrassment, shame, and a sense of failure because of her past condition. It also can be useful in helping an inexperienced woman "find her voice" in relation to her sexuality, and develop a healthy sexual self esteem. Whereas before she may have felt that she "owed" her partner intercourse and was a disappointment to her husband because she was unable to participate in this aspect of her marriage vows, once she becomes physically functional new issues may arise.

A woman can more readily consider her own sexual pleasure after vaginismus, and she can now focus not just on what might please her husband, but also what pleases or arouses her. In order to become aroused and become physically orgasmic she must focus on pleasurable sensations and physical arousal within her own body.

For a woman with a history of avoiding intercourse, achieving sexual pleasure requires releasing guilt, feelings of inadequacy, and her singular focus on what her partner might enjoy. Sex therapy can help her identify prior sexual activities that were unpleasant or only neutral, and help her begin to create new, positive, sensual associations with loveplay. Keep in mind that only 33 percent of women have orgasms from intercourse, so while vaginal penetration can be a fun option, it is not the only way to have sexual activity or experience pleasure.

Although this chapter has focused on the benefits of sex counseling for women with vaginismus, it is also important to emphasize that sex therapy has equal value for their partners. For starters, it can help the man overcome any entrenched fears of hurting his wife during intercourse. In addition, partners bring to the bed their own insecurities and lack of know-how. Even if they no longer feel they have to withhold displays of sexual affection or inhibit their overt desire, that does not mean they know exactly what to do with it!

For men and women who have weathered vaginismus, sex therapy can play a crucial role in helping them begin the process of reframing not only their incorrect self perceptions, but also their perceptions of themselves as a couple. Sex counselor Talli Rosenbaum offered the following insights on this particular issue.

"Couples often define themselves by the boundaries they have drawn and have become accustomed to. Although they are highly motivated to "step across the line," they have labeled each other and themselves as the couple who doesn't have sex for so long that this has become their default status quo.

"Changing that status becomes a source of anxiety and raises many potential questions. What if my partner can function, but I can't? What if we can do it, but it's not pleasurable? What if he or she wants to do it every night? Allowing these fears to be verbalized enables the therapeutic intervention to focus on how the dysfunction has served as a boundary, but that it is an unnecessary one, as boundaries can be established in healthier and more functional ways.[1]"

The Issue of Low Libido : "Not Tonight, Honey..."

Frustrations over low sexual desire and infrequency of lovemaking are among the most common problems that bring couples into sex therapy, and can be particularly challenging to address for women who have suffered with vaginismus. This absence of desire, clinically described as low libido, is something several of my own patients have experienced. For example, one woman who was treated successfully for vaginismus confided in me that she still has "no sex drive." After further conversation, she reported that she has "felt close to orgasm," but has "never felt the release."

Is a lack of desire in women a lingering psychological issue related to vaginismus? Is it due to the couple's sexual inexperience? Or is it a separate medical problem that needs to be diagnosed and treated as such. The fact that a low libido may be attributed to a diversity of individual or integrated psychological or physical causes—stress, fear, fatigue, body image, hormone levels, a history of abuse or negative associations with sex—makes it all the more challenging to pinpoint and treat.

A colleague of mine and an expert on the issue of libido, Bat Sheva Marcus, PhD, the clinical director of the Medical Center for Female

Sexuality in Purchase, New York, volunteered the following insights. "Our experience is that even vaginismus sufferers who have a healthy sex drive begin to resist any type of sexual encounters. If they're married or living with someone, most often their "non-intercourse" sexual encounters taper off. Every time they have sex they feel like they should try again, and it hurts or they fail. Some just feel so terrible about the situation they find it easier not to think about it, and not having sex at all is one way to do that."

Dr. Marcus added, "Those patients who have avoided any sexual contact, who, in addition to their fear of penetration, also seem to have a history characterized by a lack of interest in sex, inability to become aroused, no history of masturbation, generally continue to have those problems after penetration is possible."

Given all the diverse factors that can play a role in low libido, it is critical for practitioners to fully understand the woman's pre-intercourse sexual history as well as her masturbation history, in order to make an accurate diagnosis and develop an appropriate treatment plan. This allows the professionals to determine what, if any, psychological factors are involved with the sexual dysfunction. In cases where sexual history or relationship issues appear to be significant contributing factors, sex therapy can be hugely effective in overcoming low desire.

That said, while psychological factors often inhibit libido, the patient should also have a thorough physical examination, including blood tests to determine what, if any, physical causes are contributing to her lack of sex drive. For example, Dr. Marcus noted a frequent and clear link between raising low hormone levels and raising a woman's libido, her ability to become aroused, and the quality of her orgasms. In other words, for a woman for whom low hormones play a significant role in her lack of desire, hormone therapy can prove greatly beneficial, but without it, she may have a hard time increasing her desire.

Dr. Marcus went on to add an obvious caveat, "Higher levels of hormones probably won't make up for an abusive marriage or a failed relationship! So hormone therapy should ideally be provided by practitioners who have the time and the expertise to evaluate the totality of a patient's experience and provide guidance to her within the context of her lifestyle and current relationship."

At its essence, Dr. Marcus shared, "treatment for sexual dysfunction is a combination of science and art." There is no single optimal treatment for all patients; each plan needs to be customized to the individual based upon what works. Most important, however, is that even when the flame of desire seems non-existent, a spark can be kindled and the great majority of couples can find their own path to intimacy.

Homework for Lovers

One of the first steps toward healthy sexuality and nurturing desire is to become knowledgeable about your and your partner's bodies through education and self exploration. To that end, read educational books, with diagrams that locate body parts, to one another. Not only are you learning together but also starting to develop a comfortable sexual language.

As you feel more comfortable and safe, you can then begin to lovingly explore one another visually and with touch. A good way to start is with sensate focus activities designed to reduce anxiety and discover your and your partner's erogenous zones through non-genital touching in non-demanding situations

Below are just a few "homework" assignments that Dr. Deborah Neel offers her sex therapy clients at her practice in Raleigh, North Carolina. I suggest that you and your partner try these as well, to develop a greater awareness of your own pleasurable sensations, both when giving and receiving touch. These activities may feel awkward at first. Feel free to giggle! Try to enjoy yourself and remain open to your own and your partner's feelings and physical responses.

 Schedule a one-to-three-hour block of time one day or more each week to spend uninterrupted time together. Turn off all electronics and focus on one another. Practice "active listening" by paying full attention to your partner's words and paraphrasing back what you heard. Offer. Receive. Welcome. Accept.

 As you grow more comfortable communicating using mutually acceptable sexual language, begin to incorporate sensate focus exercises. While fully clothed, take turns caressing one another's feet or back, for example, but do not touch breasts or genitals. The goal is to practice giving, receiving, and accepting pleasurable touch.

❀ As your comfort level increases with these sensate focus exercises, remove articles of clothing and incorporate touching the breasts and genitals. If, at any point, you feel anxiety or a negative feeling, stop. Partner, please do not take any hesitancy personally! If possible, continue the connecting touch but with no motion, pausing to see if the anxiety might subside. If so, proceed with the exercise. If not, try again later.

❀ At the close of each exercise, offer your partner feedback related to how you felt emotionally and physically, both when you were the giver and the receiver of pleasure. Remember, positive and connecting experiences are the goal, not arousal or orgasm.

References:

1. Rosenbaum, T.Y. "Applying theories of social exchange and symbolic interaction in the treatment of unconsummated marriage/relationship." *Sexual and Relationship Therapy* 24, no. 1 (2009): 38-46.

Vaginismus: It's (Also) a Guy Thing

When Mikail decided to ask Mishal to marry him six months after they met, he recalled a comment she had made earlier in their relationship. "Indian girls never get a proposal like in the movies," she had lamented. Mikail explained that because they are both South Asian, there is usually a lot of family involvement in the proposal; the parents need to give their approval and there's a big engagement party. Mikail knew he wanted to ask Mishal to marry him in a more personal way. He wanted to do something fun that would give his bride-to-be her movie-worthy moment.

Mikail had just finished medical school and couldn't afford to do anything too expensive, but then he recalled that a nearby city had a university with a small planetarium on campus. With the help of the planetarium engineer, who was in on the secret, Mikail learned how to use the planetarium controls. He then created a story about how he had to go to the city for a job interview, and because he didn't know his way around, he asked Mishal to accompany him. The job interview ruse also gave him the excuse to wear a nice suit, and his lack of knowledge about the campus created a plausible reason for him to meet the "interviewer" at the easily-located campus planetarium.

While the couple waited for the interviewer to arrive at the planetarium, Mikail dimmed the lights and turned up the stars, which take a few minutes to appear in the "night sky" of the domed ceiling. Then he plugged in his MP3 player, filling the space with soft music. "Mishal was telling me to stop fiddling with everything. She thought we were going to get in trouble," he laughed. "I asked her to dance. And then I told her to look up at the stars that by now were visible, and that's where she saw the words projected onto the sky, 'Mishal, will you marry me?'"

Mikail and Mishal were both virgins when they married. While they waited until their honeymoon to try intercourse, they had enjoyed lots of cuddling and foreplay during their courtship. "We were very close physically. We enjoyed being intimate," Mikail stated. When they couldn't have sex on their wedding night they were as surprised as they were frustrated, a frustration that grew over weeks, then months, then two years.

Mikail shared that the problem was exacerbated by his own lack of sexual awareness. In his culture, he explained, sex is not a topic of discussion between parents and their children, so he was naïve about what to expect. He also worried about what the reactions might be if he confided in anyone about his sexless marriage. "For me to say to someone in my culture, 'Yeah, I've been married almost two years and have never done it'—I can't say that. The response might be, 'Oh, she's not sexual. Get rid of her.'"

Meanwhile, as a medical student training in a Western country, Mikail also felt another kind of isolation. "There's a lot of pressure and expectations for men in Western society to be dominant when it comes to sex," he said. "Here, a lot of guys are having sex when they're sixteen or seventeen years old. They have more knowledge of sexual positions. For someone like me, you become separated from that culture, especially when you're dealing with something like this condition. My friends are joking around about sex and I have to pretend I know what they're talking about. It's like that movie *The 40-Year-Old Virgin*. It's funny to a point, but for the person going through it, you feel trapped."

Mikail's background is somewhat unusual in terms of his dual perspective on Eastern and Western cultures, but his feelings as the partner of a woman with vaginismus reflect the way most of the husbands and boyfriends experience this situation. As Mikail expressed, "I was in the dark about what's normal. What isn't? How much time should it take? I thought there was something wrong with me. I felt guilty. Was I causing her to tense up? What was the issue?"

From Erection to Dejection

Most of this book has focused on the physical and psychological impact that vaginismus has on women. After all, by definition, vaginismus is a woman's disorder: an uncontrolled involuntary spasm of vaginal muscles in women who have extreme fear of any form of vaginal penetration because of pain or anticipated pain. In the medical literature, spouses of women with vaginismus are often referred to as the "pain-free" partner, yet this is far from the literal truth. Although men may be spared the physical agony of this condition, vaginismus can be emotionally damaging to both partners in the relationship, resulting in stress, anger, depression, isolation, and lost libidos.

"In the beginning it was a matter of her getting comfortable with me. She had to do a lot of focusing on relaxing her muscles. The first couple times we tried intercourse, there was a mental disconnect. Later it was more intimate but there was no pain, and no problems. Some days it's really good. Others, I get exhausted and can't sustain an erection. We're not at the point where we can try new positions. She still has a bit of hesitancy of how penetration will feel. But our sex life is starting to feel like a normal couple." – Husband of a former vaginismus patient

Even men who understand the need to take sex slowly in the beginning, and that penetration may be painful at first for women, are likely to grow frustrated and confused after multiple failed attempts at intercourse. "It's not like I expected, Bam! that first night," explained one partner of a patient. "But the next few nights and months it was the same thing over and over. I wanted to start that part of our relationship, but she retreated every time I came near her."

Most couples have never heard of vaginismus when they first experience the problem, and, therefore, they look for other reasons to explain their inability to have intercourse. The husband may assume it is all in his partner's head, that his wife is frigid, or that she is rejecting him because she is not physically attracted to him. These types of assumptions, of course, often have little if anything to do with what is really going on, yet the relationship inside and outside the bedroom can begin to deteriorate once misunderstandings like these take hold.

"My husband and I got into a lot of arguments over little things due to pent up aggression and anger over our four-year fight with vaginismus," shared another former patient. Her husband admitted that he carried a sense of shame and low self esteem because of the situation. He assumed his wife was simply rejecting him. Their anniversaries began to mark not another year of togetherness, but of battle. Over time, the couple found that the best way to cope was to avoid the issue. They poured themselves into work, cultivated a sense of numbness and guardedness, and grew emotionally distant. They had almost resigned themselves to a sexless marriage without children.

Another husband shared that his reaction was to just "shut down" after he and his wife tried and failed to have sex for several months. Despite trying again and again, they weren't making any progress. She was in excruciating pain. "I just didn't want to deal with it anymore," he explained. This particular couple had been together seven years, and married for three. They remained together, but the lack of sexual contact had taken its toll. He felt resentful. They had waited to have sex until they were married and now this! At some point, sex took on nothing but negative associations for both partners in the relationship.

Most couples consult with doctors or try several forms of treatment or therapy to address their failure at intercourse. With any kind of medical or psychological condition, seeking professional help is a natural and often productive response. But, as Mikail pointed out, even this healthy response can feel like a "double-edged sword" for the guy.

As a doctor himself, Mikail's first instinct was to encourage Mishal to seek a medical explanation for her fear of penetration. "But even that became an issue," he explained. Mishal felt guilty, pressured, and scared about seeking help. Mikail's guilt was no less. "The more I tried to convince her to see a doctor and keep trying, the more I felt like I was doing this for my own pleasure. If you push too much you feel like you are only doing it for your own gratification. It can seem really selfish."

Fortunately, many male partners agree that having the condition identified makes a big difference. "It was as if a light bulb went on," is how the husband of one patient expressed it. "Until then I had no idea. I just figured my wife was extremely tight, or that it was a conscious thing."

Understanding the psychological aspect of vaginismus allows partners to address this condition in a manner that transcends hurt feelings, blame, and anger. It is beneficial for the partners to also witness first-hand the muscle spasms that prevent intercourse. As I've mentioned, I often have the partner observe the procedure in the surgical center, looking over my shoulder as I treat the vaginal spasms that occur even after the woman is sedated.

However, even with a greater understanding of vaginismus, and even after penetration is possible, the partner may still struggle with the aftermath of this condition. For example, many of the husbands of vaginismus patients have confided that they now have problems with arousal, as well as sustaining an erection. They may remain afraid of hurting the one they love. Their history of problems with penetration may have left them squeamish. Some report they feel like they are "forcing" themselves on their partners, or that the intercourse feels clinical rather than sexy or spontaneous.

On a related note, because couples need to take it very slow when they initiate intercourse, it also can be difficult for the man to sustain an erection for the time it may take to achieve even minimal or tip-only penetration. Fortunately, the proper dose of Viagra or Cialis can help with this matter. Just make sure not to overdo it—remember the husband who was prescribed a 100mg dose of Viagra and fainted, although he was able to tolerate the drug after the dosage was reduced by half.

Another issue is that intercourse is only one part of the sexual equation. In reality, intimacy is just as important—even more so!—in creating a good sex life. This holds true as much for the man as for the woman in a relationship. One husband aptly explained, "The important part of the relationship is not just the physical aspect. What enhances the physical is if you improve the other stuff—if you have a psychological understanding of each other, knowing how the other person feels and how to react to it, knowing when the other person is upset, knowing what to say or not to say. Body language is really important—the way you touch someone, the way you hold them can make a huge difference.

"Having a good sense of humor," he added, "is also extremely important, especially with the sex part. If we take it too seriously it becomes more intimidating and the expectations are too high. All of these things take time and patience to develop in a relationship," he smiled. "That's why I go fishing."

I have nothing but admiration for the couples who continue to seek treatment for vaginismus and who refuse to give up. Most of them have weathered years of stress and anxiety over this condition. They already have committed significant amounts of time, emotional energy, and money in trying to treat this problem.

On so many levels, vaginismus is a condition that challenges even the strongest relationships. Men (and obviously women, but this is a chapter focused on the guys) have sexual needs. Most want children. If they have had sex before with other partners, this can add to the problem because they cannot help but make comparisons to their past relationships, or other "normal" couples. For some husbands, the situation becomes so intolerable that divorce seems like the only answer. For others, the guys may resort to cheating or looking for sexual release through online partners, even when they still love their wives. This behavior isn't justifiable; it just is.

However, for all the heartbreak and challenges related to this condition, there is another reality. I have seen how just as many husbands have been instrumental in helping their partners cope with this condition. They see it as not just the woman's problem but a challenge to tackle together. One woman described her husband of four years as very supportive during their sexless marriage. "I think the whole situation has brought us closer," she wrote, "and made us realize we would be happy together even if we don't have sex."

The husband of another former vaginismus patient shared similar positive feelings. He wrote to me about the unexpected "advantage" of a marriage in which there is sexual intimacy, but not intercourse. "The relationship with my wife is built upon things of substance; not just love and shared values, but we also enjoy many of the same activities and spend lots of quality time together. This is not to say that relationships that include intercourse do not have these components, but for five years ours did not have sex to leverage/lean upon, so we first built a full relationship on everything else."

Once the couples are on the other side of vaginismus, and pain-free penetration becomes possible, even shaky relationships can often change for the better in a relatively short period of time. Several partners of vaginismus patients have expressed the following sentiment: The challenge of overcoming vaginismus can do one of two things—destroy or strengthen a relationship.

A young couple who had been struggling with vaginismus for several years, to the point where it was threatening their marriage, recently obtained treatment for the condition. When they were in the recovery room for more lessons on dilation, the husband described his feelings about the procedure and their struggles with vaginismus. "To go through something like this together," he told me, the emotion obvious in his voice, "it should make us stronger in the long run." Then he reached for his wife's hand and added, "It already has."

Postscript: Mikail and Mishal were able to achieve intercourse one month after her treatment. "By about the fourth or fifth time," Mikail reported, "Mishal was able to enjoy it, as well. We finally got a good idea of the mechanics and I wasn't getting exhausted." Six months later, Mikail wrote to let me know they were expecting a boy!

Her Story : His Story

The following first-person accounts are from a married couple who have been dealing with vaginismus for over five years. While their perspectives are not meant to represent every vaginismus patient and her partner, these accounts do capture experiences and emotions typical of so many couples who find themselves living with this condition. I found the story of their journey for a cure—shared first from the wife's point of view, then from the husband's—to be enlightening and moving. I hope you do too.

Her Story

For me, all of this started when I got married. I had met my wonderful husband, Jordan, in high school. We became engaged when I was a senior, and married when I finished my third year in college. He had just finished boot camp for the United States Marine Corps. We were looking forward to a happy and loving marriage. We had waited until marriage to have sex because we are devout Christians, so we never knew there would be a problem.

The early warning signs were there: not being able to use tampons; not wanting to go through doctors' examinations. I just never put any of it together. At that point there was nothing to put together.

Needless to say, our wedding night did not go well. I made an appointment with my doctor the next day. She was kind and considerate. She perceived it all to be wedding jitters. She did not do a vaginal examination because she did not want to scare me further. Instead, she gave me a small dose of Valium and Lidocaine gel to help me in the future. She told me not to worry, that everyone goes through this their first time.

But it didn't get better. We continued to struggle. My husband felt rejected and I felt alone and ostracized. It was as if I had a ghastly scar on my face. I felt marked, as though everyone around me could see my shame. The only other person who knew what I was going through was my mother, and she did not know what to make of it either. Not having much faith in men, my mother advised that I grin and bear it, and get over this quickly or my husband would divorce me. She said sex is everything to a man; he won't put up with this for long.

My husband and I handled things the best we could. Our first year of marriage was rocky. I kept asking for help and was constantly pushed to the side. I saw four doctors, all part of my primary care team, before I was referred to gynecology. Some of the advice I got was to widen the vaginal opening by using vaginal weights; small dildos; even candles. Do not try this last one. I was informed by another doctor how the candle wax can rub off, cake and trap bacteria, leading to monstrous infections.

I spent two years being bounced around to different doctors. I was sent to family therapy, personal therapy, and hypnotherapy, until someone stopped and really listened to what I was describing. Sadly most doctors, even the gynecologists, had never heard of vaginismus.

I don't want to sound ungrateful. Most of these doctors were doing their best to figure out what was wrong with me. Each of the therapies had its own benefits. Hypnotherapy, especially. We learned that I, probably most of my life, had been using my Kegel muscles as my tension release. Every time I was stressed or scared I would clench those muscles like other people clench their teeth. We then worked to replace that with another reaction. I don't clench there anymore.

Dr. A. was the first doctor to identify what was wrong with me. She had a mild form of vaginismus herself in younger years, and she put me on the path to proper treatment. She was the first to recommend dilation therapy. She also did a biopsy and Pap test under anesthesia to make sure I was internally normal. She explained everything to both me and my husband. About this time, I let my mom in on what was going on with me. For the last three years I'd let her assume that I had worked it out with my husband and things were fine. I had been too embarrassed and ashamed to tell her the truth.

After six months it was clear I had failed dilation therapy. I felt guilty and ashamed. I did try to do what the doctor asked, but I felt like I was stabbing myself in the worst possible place, and every instinct I had railed against what I was doing. Even just the sight or thought of the dilators caused waves of anxiety, nausea, and guilt. I cried a lot.

I went to see one specialist after another. Some were convinced I was sexually abused and wanted me in therapy; others didn't want to treat me at all. The last specialist I saw was probably the worst. He forced me through a pelvic examination. Then, as if that wasn't enough, he asked if I could handle a rectal examination. I told him that I didn't think I could and that I didn't want to try. I'd already had enough for one day. He said I would be fine and did it anyway. Even the nurse looked uncomfortable, but said nothing. After it was finally over, he said he didn't know how to help me. I had already done his treatment plan; the only thing he could offer was more counseling. He didn't even want to accept me as a patient. I was floored!

I cried all the way home. My husband was appalled when I told him what happened. I didn't know what to do. There was nowhere left to send me and I had no help. I went into a bad depression after that. I stopped going to the gym, to church. I didn't go out at all unless I had to. I felt hopeless. I felt like there was no future for me. My husband wouldn't put up with this forever. We both wanted children and there was just no hope for that now.

I had also wanted my grandfather to know his great grandchildren. He's a genealogist, and I'm his only granddaughter. He is all about family and legacy, and is convinced he will be forgotten when he dies. I wanted to give him a namesake and for him to hold that child in his arms, to know we won't forget him. How could I do that now? All I could see were years ticking by, and our dreams for a family going with them.

It was my husband who found Dr. Pacik's website and had me call the next day. The first person I spoke to was Gloria, one of the medical assistants. She was sweet and welcoming. I told her my diagnosis and for the first time I wasn't asked to explain it! Then I was transferred to Ellen, a surgical technologist. I told her about some of my experiences, how long things had been like this, how badly we wanted children and felt like there was nothing left to try. She said she believed they could help me. I made a tentative appointment and started getting ready to travel to New Hampshire. Ellen sent me information on others I could talk with about this disorder, and links to websites and videos, just to let me know I wasn't alone.

The weeks passed more quickly than I realized, and, before long, it was September and time to go. My husband could not get off work to come with me so Mom and I went to meet Dr. Pacik. The flight was quick and easy. I didn't start to get nervous until we reached the hotel that night. I had a hard time sleeping, and I was scared the next morning.

We arrived at Dr. Pacik's office at 7 a.m. and the first one to greet me was Gloria, the person with the sweet voice I had spoken with over the phone. I was calm for a while. Then Dr. Pacik came and introduced himself. He was wonderful and reminded me a lot of my grandfather. He explained what was going to happen. The procedure would be happening in just a few minutes! Now I was scared again.

Mom and I were given a tour of the practice and taken to the recovery room where I met Nurse Barbara. She was so kind. I cannot express how much of a comfort her bright cheery demeanor was! She got me my gown to change into and rubber-soled socks, and put me in a bed with a fuzzy purple heating blanket. It was all I could do not to sing, "one-eyed, one-horned, giant purple people eater!"

Soon after that I was taken to the surgical room and put to sleep. The anesthesiologist was very friendly and had me out before I knew what was going on. I don't even remember walking to the surgical room. Mom stayed with me the whole time and the procedure went perfectly.

I woke up under the warm "people eater" blanket. There were two other women there, too. They had just gone through the same procedure and had their husbands with them. I already had the pink dilator in place. I was really amazed. Pink is the second largest dilator, something I couldn't have hoped to insert before the Botox procedure. And the funny thing was that the Botox hadn't even taken effect yet.

Mom sat beside me while Barbara, the nurse, was buzzing around me and the two other patients. We also now had Ellen who helped us learn how to remove, move, and put the dilator into place that first day before we went back to our motel. The next day and a half, we moved down one size to the purple dilator. I won't lie and say it was fun, easy, or even comfortable, but I could do it and it wasn't excruciating, as it had been in the past. Ellen, Barbara, and Dr. Pacik were a world of encouragement. I never once felt embarrassed or alone.

The second day was probably the hardest for me. I was sore from all the work from the day before and I had slept with the dilator in place that night. Believe it or not, this was not as hard as you think. Sleeping with the dilator became a great way for me to do my physical therapy. It gave me eight hours of solid time dilating, and I had very little discomfort. I stayed with the purple dilator most of that second day, but Ellen and Dr. Pacik wanted all of us who'd had the procedure that same day (my "Botox Buddies" were from Britain and California) to move back up to the bigger pink dilator before we left New Hampshire.

The pink dilator was slow getting into place and it didn't want to stay, but I was able to leave it in for a few hours at a time, although sitting was uncomfortable. Mom and I saw some of the town that third day, and all of us were invited to Dr. Pacik's house for dinner that night. It was a lot of fun. We met his wife and really got to know one another over the course of the evening. We talked about our families, our history with this disorder, our husbands, and our progress since coming for the procedure. All of us had made real progress! (We are still in contact with each other to this day.)

I stayed with the pink dilator through that night and our last therapy day, but went down to purple to travel home. I was desperate not to lose the progress I had made. Working with the dilators at home was the real test. The Botox had started working and made dilation a lot easier. Mom stayed with us for a few days. Having her support along with my husband's was a real blessing. Dr. Pacik, Ellen, and Gloria kept in contact with me every couple of weeks.

For the first few weeks I would dilate all night, and as long as I could during the day (four to six hours) with the pink dilator. But I did make the mistake of forgetting to keep the dilator well lubricated and ended up hurting myself somewhat. Having it in so long often left me feeling bruised. Ellen said I was probably overdoing it. I had to dilate a little less often and with the purple dilator for a little over a week. That was very frustrating for me, but when I went back to the pink dilator it went in easily. I toned down my regimen to dilating at night and two-to-three hours a day. For the first month I didn't even want to try sex. First, I had to get over a lot of fear and aversion to the whole process, but I made it!

Around the middle of my second month after the procedure, my husband and I tried sex. Dr. Pacik told us not to expect too much, and not to even try for actual "sex" the first few times. He said just to take it slow, at our own pace. I was downright scared, so much so I was shaking and couldn't stop or calm down. I was afraid of failing and my husband being disappointed in me or angry. I also was afraid of pain. My husband listened to my fears and told me not to worry. He said he was so proud of how far I had come and even if we didn't have sex right away, we were trying and working toward that goal. We would get there.

We did it!!! The first time was clumsy and very slow. I had some really uncomfortable places that needed more work but I didn't freak out, and I wasn't in pain. We did it twice that night and the second time I was able to take more movement and penetration. I was so relieved and happy. I felt hope for the first time in a long time! Maybe now we really could have a family. My husband said he loved me and was so very proud of me!

For the first two-and-a-half months (give or take a little) I dilated daily, all night, and thirty minutes before sex. My husband and I got better and better. Then I went down to dilating at night and before sex. I did try for a while to move up to blue (the largest dilator) but though I could get it into place and keep it in for an hour or so, it was never something I could do continuously. I found that the pink dilator worked well for me and my husband, and we didn't need to go up anymore.

By December I was actually enjoying sex some of the time and able to do it without anxiety. My husband and I have come a long way. The Botox has worn off and I am not dilating as much anymore simply because I don't have to. YAY!!! I hope to get to the point where I don't need to dilate at all. Then I will say I'm cured. For now I am thrilled with the progress I have made and know I will reach my goal in time. I made it from no penetration to sex in three months. I can make it all the way.

P.S. Jordan and I are doing great. Oh and by the way, it is now April (six months since my procedure) and I am four months pregnant with our first child!!! Everyone is ecstatic! Mom cried when I told her. The family is calling the baby "Peanut" because of the ultrasound photo. We find out in three weeks if we are having a boy or girl.

His Story

My name is Jordan. I am a combat engineer in the United States Marine Corps. I met my wife in high school. I was a freshman and brand new to JROTC. She was issuing the uniforms and I "ma'amed" her to death. We started dating in my sophomore year and kept dating the rest of high school. We had decided not to have sex prior to marriage because of our faith.

On our wedding night we were unable to consummate our marriage due to what I thought at the time was my blushing bride's nerves. However, after several months, I began to actually despise her. It was emasculating, and I thought and said several terrible things, even though I wanted to stay patient and work with her. I love my wife and even though I felt rejected I didn't want to lose her. She was having a hard enough time with the doctors and her own guilt of failure.

I was determined to be able to make love to my wife before I deployed to Iraq for the first time. I deployed in August 2006. It didn't happen. Then I thought surely before my second deployment in October 2008. I almost divorced her over all of this. I caused countless fights, and was an embarrassment to myself. Did she just not want me? Or was she really having a problem the doctors couldn't find? What about kids and family? Could I really deal with this my whole life?

I was at my wit's end. We had gone to countless doctors, from those working in general medicine to specialists and head shrinks, even a hypnotherapist. Nothing helped over two-and-a-half years of trying. Then a doctor suggested it could be vaginismus, and again told us that dilation was the only option with the same old rigid, plastic dilators. One sex therapist even told us to use candles. (Yeah, it didn't work.) My wife tried self medication with wine and even sleeping pills, but when we tried to have sex it was like trying to push against a brick wall. Not happening.

After two more years of doctors and failed treatments, my wife gave up and went into a bad depression. Needless to say, I was very worried. So with no other option I turned to Google and read several articles. One feminist website told me I was basically a sexist pig for trying to have sex with my wife, and that I could have a "whole" marriage without sex. Then I found it, an article about Dr. Pacik's work. I went to my wife and showed her. We were both skeptical, but felt a glimmer of hope.

We called Dr. Pacik's office and spoke with the surgical technologist, Ellen. She explained the treatment and that Botox was just one part of the program. She emphasized the importance of working with the dilators, knowing how to use them, as well as the importance of my wife knowing her body. The treatment really sounded different, but my wife seemed hopeful. She was impressed with the staff and their overall knowledge of the condition. I read Dr. Pacik's website articles on vaginismus. For the first time I actually started to understand what my wife was going through, what vaginismus really is. I wish I had understood this years ago.

I was unable to go to New Hampshire with my wife for the procedure due to work commitments, but she came home having made two new friends she e-mails regularly. (And my bride never talks to people, over e-mail, phone, or otherwise.) She explained to me how important the "whole" treatment was and gave me my "To Do" list from Dr. Pacik. (Go slow. Help with the dilators. Start with "tip only" penetration…)

It was amazing. Within the second month I was actually able to penetrate my wife for the first time. We both wept. It was slow at first, but within a couple weeks we were able to get more…adventuresome. On January 4, 2010, we found out that she is pregnant!!!

Though sex is not necessary for a successful marriage, it can be a vital part. Now that we are able to make love, I feel closer to my wife than ever before.

Putting the "Fun" in Functional

You've probably seen lots of scenes in movies that play out something like this. The man and woman look at each other longingly for about two seconds. Next comes a blur of clothes being pushed aside or discarded, some intense thrusting during intercourse, a lot of loud moaning, and then, maybe half a minute after it all started, both partners crescendo to orgasm at exactly the same time.

Ah, only in the movies.

Scenes like these give all couples, not just those who have had to overcome the issue of vaginismus, the wrong idea about sex, the human anatomy, and the art of lovemaking. Consider just this one often-held misconception—that intercourse leads to orgasm in women. In fact, only 20 to 30 percent of women climax with intercourse. Armed with this knowledge, both you and your partner can avoid feeling like failures if you don't climax, let alone climax simultaneously, with penetration and thrusting.

For all couples, the difference between sex and good sex can depend on many things, including trust, open communication, and an understanding of your partner's and your own erogenous zones. Despite the fact that sex is a natural act, every couple needs to cultivate the physical and emotional aspects to a good sexual relationship.

But for couples who have struggled with vaginismus and are now able to have intercourse, the learning curve may be even steeper than average.

This is understandable, given that most women and their partners who have lived with this condition are sexually underdeveloped. Most of the women have never even had the luxury of intercourse, let alone the opportunity to discover their own sexual preferences. Their partners also may be virgins or simply inexperienced. Even if they have had numerous premarital partners, they may not understand the concept of intimate companionship in combination with the physical act of intercourse.

"Now, five years into our marriage, sex has been introduced in its full glory. We are able to take a stable and happy relationship and inject something new, intimate, and sexy. While some of our friends are looking for ways to rekindle the spark, we have a five-alarm fire on our hands." – Husband of a former vaginismus patient

In addition, even after the pain of penetration is no longer an issue, there may remain a lingering fear and aversion to intimacy. Botox may act like a wonder drug in terms of its effectiveness in treating vaginal spasms, but it takes more than Botox to eliminate the emotional obstacles that can inhibit intimacy; obstacles ranging from a negative body image to entrenched associations that equate sex with pain or "dirty" behavior.

Complicating matters even further, couples who have lived with vaginismus often have a history of bickering and disconnect that has its roots in years of frustration. The tension may have started in the bedroom thanks to this condition, but often ends up permeating the entire relationship. In my years of treating women with vaginismus, I have seen a fair share of couples on the brink of divorce. A case in point: one of my patients returned home after her three-day treatment only to be served divorce papers. Even more common, I have treated many couples that remain together, but live as brother and sister or roommates, as one patient's husband described their relationship.

Given all the factors that can get in the way of healthy sexuality and just plain good sex, it's no surprise that, in some cases, women who have had vaginismus, and/or their partners, often have low or even indiscernible libidos. At times, it may feel preferable for the woman, even after her vaginismus is cured, to just let go of her sexuality, to think, *Well, at least I can function now…or at least I got my baby…or at least I can make my husband happy…*

Because the sex drives of women with vaginismus may have waned over the years or been low to begin with, some sex counselors and doctors are cautious, even skeptical that this can be fully overcome. They point to scattered studies that suggest women with vaginismus can be "cured," but few go on to enjoy long-term meaningful sexual relationships. I encounter this stance frequently when talking with therapists or submitting articles to editors at professional journals, despite what I see with my patients as many positive signs to the contrary.

My feelings about this issue are this: Similar to how women with vaginismus have "normal" vaginas that can function just fine once their vaginismus is cured, I suspect that most of them also have "normal" libidos that can be developed and nurtured to allow them to experience a fulfilling sexuality or at least sensuality with a partner. I am convinced that both practitioners and patients need to be wary of writing off too soon "the return of desire," to borrow the title phrase of a valuable book on rediscovering your sexual passion by Dr. Gina Ogden.

To help my vaginismus patients feel more sexually confident, my staff and I make a point to provide aftercare that includes counseling about building the kind of trust necessary to open yourself up, discover your erogenous zones, and define intimacy on your own terms.

In addition, I am a strong advocate of couples working with a sex therapist after successful treatment of vaginismus with Botox injections. For many of my patients, the Botox procedure and/or indwelling dilator allow for a momentous triumph that not only opens the door to intercourse, but also enables them to now be truly receptive to the benefits of clinical sex counseling for quality of life, mental health, and relationship issues. The impossible task of following counseling suggestions before treatment now becomes possible, and treated patients are able to embrace recommendations made by their therapist. At this point, therapists believe in their clients' ability to follow therapeutic assignments without the resistance that was difficult to overcome prior to treatment with Botox.

Putting the Fun in Functional: My Top 10 Tips

I am not a certified sex therapist, but I have discovered that for many former vaginismus patients, just a little information and guidance can go a long way in helping them begin to establish true intimacy with their partners. In fact, even just giving couples "permission" to have fun and experiment may be all that it takes to spark their own ideas and sexual creativity.

What follows is a list of suggestions that my staff and I offer to treated patients who have become sexually "functional," but understandably want more from their intimate relationships than simply pain-free intercourse. Admittedly, for some former vaginismus sufferers, these suggestions won't be enough, especially if there are deeper issues related to intimacy and intercourse that need to be addressed. Regardless, I hope all readers will be able to use these suggestions to some degree to improve intimacy with their partners, and eventually move beyond what is possible to what is pleasurable.

(Note: For those readers interested in additional references specifically related to desire, intimacy, and long-term sexual satisfaction, please see the Recommended Reading list at the back of this book.)

1. Self pleasuring. Pleasuring your own body is a big leap for many women with vaginismus; not surprisingly most of my patients have never touched themselves "down there," and many are unfamiliar with their own anatomy. That's why self-pleasuring is important as a teaching tool, as well as a source of enjoyment. Self stimulation, usually in the form of massaging or rubbing the clitoris and vulva, gives you a way to feel comfortable and in control. And once you discover what feels good, from angles to degree of pressure to intensity of clitoral stimulation, you can communicate all of this to your partner, as well.

2. Think above and below the waist. Many areas of your body, not just the clitoris or vulva, can respond to loving and sexual stimulation. How about a foot massage? Or have your partner experiment by caressing your breasts, scalp, ears, neck, and back. Does his touch in any of these areas turn you on? Massaging many different places of the body is a great form of foreplay, or a pleasurable end in and of itself.

First Comes Orgasm...Then Intercourse

Below is an excerpt from the book *A Tired Woman's Guide to Passionate Sex: Regain Your Desire and Reignite Your Relationship* by psychologist Laurie Mintz. This passage addresses the myths and pressure women feel in regard to intercourse and orgasm.

The traditional definition of foreplay is the caressing that takes place before intercourse. Such wording implies that touching prior to intercourse is useful only as a lead-in to the main event, with the main event being intercourse. Given that most men orgasm during intercourse and that, according to the Hite Report, 70 percent of women don't orgasm during intercourse, this is a male-defined way of talking about sex. Some sex experts, and some women I talk to, say it works best if the woman can have an orgasm separate from intercourse. A few go further to say that this works best if the woman's orgasm occurs before intercourse. If these women were defining the words, the clitoral caressing (and orgasm) that occurs before intercourse would be called sex and intercourse would be called post-play. Sex expert Lori Buckley prefers the term "sex play" to foreplay, pointing out that that clitoral stimulation (by oneself, one's partner, or a vibrator) can occur before, during, after, or even instead of, intercourse.

This is not to say that women don't like intercourse. Lots of women enjoy intercourse tremendously. It is just that the vast majority of women require clitoral stimulation to orgasm. For women, the orgasm "hot button" is the clitoris. The clitoris has more nerve endings than anywhere else in the body. Learning this helped one of my very religious clients get comfortable with asking her husband to stimulate her clitoris. "After all," she said, "I think my clitoris must be God's gift for me. He put all those nerve endings there for a reason."

During intercourse, the clitoris is only indirectly stimulated and this is why only a minority of women orgasm through penetration alone. Those women who do orgasm through penetration alone often say they do so in the woman-on-top position; this may be because of the friction of rubbing the clitoris against one's partner's abdomen or the shaft of his penis. Another theory is that women who have orgasms during intercourse have clitorises that are closer to their vagina than those who do not. The bottom line is that in order for a woman to reach orgasm, she generally must have her clitoris in contact with something and it must be stimulated.

3. Do some serious kissing. Or get naked. Or just touch one another. But commit beforehand to going no further. Setting boundaries like this up front is a great way to build trust, and set a solid foundation for intimacy before trying intercourse…or at any point during your sexual relationship.

4. Turn on together. Watching erotic movies or porn, or reading aloud sexy novels can be a valid way to tune in and turn on together. Or how about some erotic poetry? A quick online search reveals a host of options. Some sites offer mild eroticism, some explicit, but with so much variety you're bound to find something to suit your tastes. Related to this, talk about your fantasies. Instead of feeling threatened, many couples enjoy hearing about their partners' sexual turn-ons. This kind of entertainment isn't right for everybody, but for a lot of couples this kind of shared activity can provide a good source of ideas for sex play, and get you both in the mood at the same time.

5. Go shopping. And I don't mean for groceries. Every now and then, consider dressing up for your man and for yourself in pretty or revealing lingerie. Sexy outfits can be a turn-on for both partners in the relationship. Just making the effort to look enticing invites intimacy because it shows that you value your sexual relationship.

6. Fill Your Toy Box. As a way of getting to know your pleasure spots, a vibrator is a terrific enhancement whether you're masturbating or making love. Then, after you grow more comfortable using a vibrator on your own body or inviting your partner to do so, you can always invest in a few more sex toys that add variety and keep things playful.

7. Pose for pix. Why not visit a professional photographer for some glamour shots of yourself, and give the photos to your lover as a special gift. By doing so, you're also likely to see your own body in a new light and yourself as a sensuous, desirable woman. Another small gesture that can make a big difference is to display a special photo of you and your partner in a prominent place. The photo doesn't even need to be sexy, just loving. For example, I have a picture of my wife hugging me at the end of a dock, with the Gulf of Mexico in the background. Every time I look at that picture I feel a renewed love and appreciation for her, an intimacy that transcends the bedroom.

8. Make a point to have date nights. I'm sure you've heard this one before. But it really can make a difference. Just spending time alone with your partner, outside of the household and away from work and everyday worries, can set the stage for easy conversation and remind you of why you were attracted to each other in the first place. And don't think the "date" has to be candles and an expensive dinner. Go to an amusement park, or fishing, or any place fun that takes the pressure off performing.

9. Discuss your needs for "sex for release" versus "sex for intimacy." This distinction is particularly important for couples who either have differences in desire, or where one or both have a high need for sex for release, which can be achieved through masturbation, for example, and a low-to-moderate need for sex for intimacy. While one partner may not always be responsible for taking care of the other partner's sexual needs or desired frequency for orgasms, it is the responsibility of each person in the relationship to work to make sure that their own and their partner's need for intimacy are being met.

10. Schedule sex on a regular basis. In today's hectic world, sex can easily drop to the bottom of your "To Do" list unless you make it a priority. So pick a date, morning, noon, or night, and make love-making, with or without intercourse, a consistent and promised part of your ongoing relationship.

EPILOGUE

PARTING THE CURTAIN:
THE VOICES OF VAGINISMUS

...I myself have had times where I've cried continuously because it seems that no one could possibly understand what I was going through. I carried the weight on my shoulders alone because I didn't want to burden anyone. I felt like they would just get tired of hearing me talk about "my problem." I am so thankful to know that I have been wrong about myself all of these years. I am not a failure (and neither are you). I am not less of a woman because of vaginismus (and neither are you). And, most importantly, I am not alone (and neither are you).
— From an e-mail exchange between a former and a current vaginismus sufferer

...The most important thing is you're making progress. Yay!!! It's a continuous road for all three of us no matter where we are at this time. We have to keep working and celebrate small wins and big wins along the way. I am so thankful because you both know exactly how I feel. You understand that using a tampon is getting easier and penetration is uncomfortable but it can and will work. So hooray to us all! The journey is tough but well worth it. Peace, love, and great sex!
— From an e-mail exchange between three vaginismus patients recently treated on the same day

My involvement in the treatment of vaginismus has been an amazing part of my professional journey, most notably in the fact that it has brought a diversity of extraordinary women to my practice. I continue to be moved by the courage and determination women with vaginismus have demonstrated in confronting this challenging condition. They have endured considerable misunderstanding, blame, and self-doubt. They have had to find answers on their own. They have also taught me volumes about vaginismus—from how to treat it, to how far the medical community at large still has to go in terms of listening, really listening, to women with sexual pain.

But of all the things my vaginismus patients have taught me over the past several years, one of the most powerful lessons I have learned is this: the worst kind of suffering is that which is done in silence.

Vaginismus receives relatively scant public attention, even though the incidence rate of women with vaginismus is as high as 7 percent of the female population, about the same as that of men with erectile dysfunction. While we cannot turn on the evening news or fire up our e-mail without an advertisement appearing for Viagra (in fact, one just popped up on my computer screen a few moments ago), we are hard-pressed to find any mention, let alone a cure, for vaginismus on network television.

The result of this dearth of attention and silence—as if painful sex is not just an embarrassing subject but a taboo one, at that—is that countless women with vaginismus feel isolated in their condition. As such, a difficult situation is made even worse as these women bear the burden of what feels like a shameful secret.

A Call to the Medical Community

The time has come to bring the study of vaginismus to the forefront of women's sexual health. While notable research continues to be done to further awareness of other female sexual pain disorders, now is the time to recognize that vaginismus needs equal attention from the medical community. Vaginismus is not a secondary condition to other types of vulvar pain and vulvodynia, and it should not be viewed or researched as such. An entity unto itself, and one that affects millions of women worldwide, this condition merits a body of research all its own.

Currently, I am continuing my own pilot study focused on the treatment of vaginismus, the parameters of which have been the subject of this book. In August 2010, I received FDA approval to study the treatment of vaginismus with Botox and progressive dilation under anesthesia. As I have enthusiastically noted, the results of my practice and this study strongly suggest that the use of Botox injections in combination with a long-acting local anesthetic and an indwelling dilator are key components to the effective treatment of vaginismus.

Yet even with such dramatic and promising results, this is only the beginning of the search for the most effective treatment for vaginismus. What exactly is the role of Botox in treating this condition? Is it really the missing link—the answer to stopping vaginal spasms once and for all? Can the same successful outcomes be achieved by using an indwelling dilator without Botox? What role does counseling play in a treatment program? How can we prevent vaginismus in the first place?

My goal is to follow up my current pilot study with Botox with a randomized controlled trial, comparing identical treatment protocols. This means that in one randomly chosen group of patients a placebo such as saline would be injected, while the other group would receive Botox. All the other parts of the treatment program would remain the same, allowing a different level of evidence-based medicine.

Ideally, of course, this type of study should extend far beyond my practice, and the number of patients within these trials would be large enough to produce significant statistical data. Even in the course of writing this book, I have been pleased to note that an increasing number of my well respected colleagues are now conducting vaginismus-related research studies of their own. Together, we can and will make progress in defeating this debilitating condition!

Organizing a Grass Roots Movement

Clearly, the medical community must do its part to initiate a greater understanding of vaginismus and how to treat it. But if seismic progress is to be made sooner rather than later, it likely needs to be driven by the women who suffer directly from this disorder. Fortunately, a model already exists that demonstrates what can be accomplished when women with a common medical issue band together and take action.

The National Vulvodynia Association (NVA) came into being in 1994. It was started by just five women with vulvodynia who decided to stop feeling isolated in their condition, and start dismantling road blocks to treatment. Today, from that grass roots movement, the NVA has become an international organization representing thousands of women. It distributes educational materials and uses its powers of advocacy to obtain significant research grants. One of the first grants was awarded to Dr. Bernard Harlow and Dr. Elizabeth Stewart, who were able to determine that up to 16 percent of women of all ages and ethnic and racial backgrounds suffer from vulvodynia.

Imagine what could be accomplished with an organization of similar scope devoted specifically to the treatment of vaginismus. Just as the National Vulvodynia Association grew from a few committed founders to a powerhouse of change, so too could a National Vaginismus Society use its collective power to lobby Congress for funding for research, as well as create a much needed public awareness campaign.

Perhaps the stirrings of such a national or even global organization are taking root among the handful of online communities that already exist for women with vaginismus. While some of these groups are open only to women with the condition, a few sites are now available to the general public and the medical community. Two such public websites are the Vaginismus Awareness Network, www.vaginismus-awareness-network.org, a non-profit site offering information on vaginismus from women who've made the journey from suffering to cured, and www.vaginismus.com. Subscription-based groups for sufferers, partners, and medical professionals can also be found at health.groups.yahoo.com/group/vaginismus.

While these groups can serve as a lifeline to women out there desperate for information on vaginismus, I would also encourage members of these groups and all women with this condition to look to the model of the National Vulvodynia Association as a way to further broaden educational efforts, treatment advocacy, and partnership with the medical community.

Dear...

Below are a few more excerpts from written exchanges between patients.

...I would never have thought in a million years that I would be able to do such a thing, but there I was inserting dilators in my body. It was an amazing experience and I would not take it back for anything in the world. You have more strength inside of you than you have ever given yourself credit for and I believe with my whole heart that you will do just fine and be amazed at what you accomplish in as little as even 24 hours...

...I enjoy being able to share because I know that it can be a bit scary facing the unknown. I was very nervous about the procedure. My boyfriend was there with me, which helped to calm me a great deal. For me, I felt as though I was somewhat okay until I had actually undressed, got in the bed downstairs, and was about to get my IV. I have no problem with needles, but it was just at that moment that a flood of emotions went through me. I knew that once I had the IV, there was no turning back. This was really going to happen. Would this procedure work for me? Wow, this could really be it. I will no longer have to feel worthless because I can't have sex...

...Thank you for your e-mail. The responses from so many of you have been overwhelming in a very positive way. I am excited as I leave for the U.S. tomorrow morning. I am a little bit nervous already. I'm actually not too worried about the procedure itself. I am much more worried about using dilators. I have never used a tampon and gynecological exams are painful. How difficult was it for you to get accustomed to using a dilator? Weren't you afraid of it at all? Hopefully I can share my success as well soon :-)

You Are Not Alone

The recovery room in my surgi-center is sectioned into three spaces, each outfitted with a bed with a heated blanket, and enclosed with full-length drapes for privacy. As you have already learned, we often treat two or three women with vaginismus on the same day. After they return to the recovery room, we make a point to request permission to open the curtains that divide them so that they can talk to one another about their experiences, fears, and expectations.

For so many of these women, having this chance to meet and talk face-to-face with other women with vaginismus is a revelation. Suddenly, they no longer see themselves as self-described "freaks" or "different in a bad way" just because they have this condition. For some, the bonds they forge in that room over the two or three days they come together for this procedure carry over long after they have returned to their homes in other states and other countries.

Knowing what a difference it makes to have someone to talk with about this condition has motivated many of our patients to reach out to others. A few of these women have chosen to publically acknowledge and discuss their vaginismus, posting their experiences on my own practice's website, or sharing their journey and insights on YouTube videos or their own blogs. And several of my past and present patients, as you have just read, generously extended their permission for me to use their words and stories in this book, though their names have all been changed or omitted to protect patient confidentially.

I believe that for the majority of women afflicted with vaginismus, reading true accounts by other women who have struggled themselves with this condition and overcome it can be enormously helpful and inspirational. The exception may be for the smaller percentage of vaginismus sufferers for whom transition to sex from dilators has been difficult, or who have more complicated cases or other problems in their relationships. In these cases, talking to women who have quickly overcome vaginismus may feel discouraging at first. But even then, with the right sensitivity and language, these women can come to recognize that they too are perfectly normal, and that different women make progress at different paces.

At the beginning of this chapter, I mentioned that one of the most powerful lessons I have learned in treating women with vaginismus is how devastating it can be to suffer in silence. As this book comes to a close, I would like to now share one last lesson that my patients with vaginismus have taught me. And that is this: When we reach out to each other, when we find the courage to share our experiences and pain, amazing things can happen.

In my practice I have seen time and time again what happens when the curtain that separates women with vaginismus is, quite literally, drawn open. My intention with this book is to serve a similar purpose. These pages are meant to part the curtain that isolates vaginismus sufferers far beyond the walls of my practice's recovery room.

If you suffer from vaginismus, if sex seems impossible and you are losing hope, let this book and the voices of the women who shared their stories within it speak to you loud and clear: You are not alone. You do not need to suffer in silence. And you can get the kind of support and help you need to overcome this condition.

Recommended Reading

A Tired Woman's Guide to Passionate Sex: Reclaim Your Desire and Reignite Your Relationship by Laurie B. Mintz (Adams Media, 2009). In this accessible guide, psychologist Laurie Mintz offers solutions for women with low sex drives caused by exhaustion, multi-tasking, stress, parenting, life... Bolstered with case studies, readers will find plenty of sympathy, insights, and worthwhile exercises.

Female Sexual Pain Disorders: Evaluation and Management by Andrew Goldstein, Caroline Pukall and Irwin Goldstein (Wiley-Blackwell, 2009). The first book devoted to the diagnosis and treatment of sexual pain in women, this work evaluates and distinguishes the causes of sexual pain in women, and differentiates the many forms of sexual pain, including conditions such as vulvodynia and vaginismus where the cause is usually unknown. All proceeds from this book are being donated to the International Society for the Study of Women's Sexual Health.

Finding the Doorbell: Sexual Satisfaction for the Long Haul by Cindy Pierce and Edie Thys Morgan (Nomad Press, 2008). Meaningful and entertaining, this book shares other people's intimate encounters and offers perspective on what is normal for the average healthy adult. The book, which dispels common false assumptions, such as that size alone matters and that great sex has to be wild, helps both partners overcome ordinary anxieties about sex, and paves the way for long-term sexual fulfillment.

Secret Suffering: How Women's Sexual and Pelvic Pain Affects Their Relationships by Susan Bilheimer and Robert J. Echenberg, MD (Greenwood Publishing Group, 2009). Women with sexual and pelvic pain and their partners talk candidly about their experiences, including the difficulties of working with the medical community. The book also shows the promise of a new, far more accepting medical paradigm of chronic pelvic and sexual pain. The appendix offers tips to relieve sexual and pelvic pain.

The Book of Love: Every Couple's Guide to Emotional and Sexual Intimacy by Laura Berman, PhD (DK Adult, 2010). Written by one of the country's most renowned sex and relationship therapists, *The Book of Love* offers information on how you and your partner can become more connected, communicative, stable, romantic, and sexually-satisfied. The book also features photographs of couples of different ages and different body types.

The Guide to Getting It On, 6th Edition by Paul Joannides and Daerick Gross Sr. (Goofy Foot Press, 2009). This book has earned rave reviews for its entertaining and enlightening insights and instruction on sex.

The Return of Desire: A Guide to Rediscovering Your Sexual Passion by Gina Ogden (Trumpeter, 2008). A seasoned sex therapist and researcher, Dr. Ogden offers a gentle and practical book on how to "Open up to the four energies that spark desire. Create heart-to-heart communication with your partner. Transcend guilt, shame, and 'good-girls-don't' messages. Help heal the sexual wounds of abuse, addiction, affairs, and low self-esteem. And enjoy sexual pleasure throughout your life."

The V Book: A Doctor's Guide to Complete Vulvovaginal Health by Elizabeth G. Stewart, MD, and Paula Spencer (Bantam, 2002). Stewart is a clinical gynecologist specializing in vulvovaginal care and a Harvard Medical School instructor. Spencer is a journalist focusing on women's and family issues. This easy-to-read guide discusses "that part" of your body. "Vagina is hardly a household word," says Dr. Stewart. *The V Book* covers vulvovaginal anatomy and functions, medical conditions, sexual issues, and more.

Acknowledgements

I count my blessings every day I go to work with such a dedicated staff. My blessings also extend to colleagues outside my practice, and to my wonderful family and friends. With much gratitude, I would like to acknowledge the following people:

Gloria Smith, our medical assistant, is the first person our prospective patients talk to when they contact our office. Her warm and supportive nature embodies the spirit of our practice, and makes every patient feel welcome and more relaxed.

As a certified surgical technologist, Ellen Wilson-Giancola is my "right arm" in the operating room and during non-surgical procedures. Her insights have contributed greatly to the development of our comprehensive treatment program for vaginismus, and to the coordinated care of all our patients.

Our former recovery room nurse Barbara Barry is a consummate professional whose skills and smile greatly enhanced the comfort of our patients. I wish her well in her new endeavors. I also would like to welcome back to the practice Andrea Popp-Connolly, always an excellent nurse and now, a new mom.

Pammy Alter, a certified surgical technologist, has been a valued assistant during countless procedures in our surgi-center. I am equally grateful for her relentless efforts to represent patients for insurance reimbursement.

My gratitude goes back over eight years to Cynthia David, MLS, MPS. As a health sciences librarian at Catholic Medical Center in Manchester, New Hampshire, Cynthia's expertise, and tireless response to my reprint needs, have seen me through the writing of many research papers.

My thanks extend to the American Board Certified anesthesiologists from Elliot Hospital who lend their talents to the care of my patients in surgery and in the recovery room. A special thanks to Dr. Richard Spaulding, whose passion for creating a healing environment is only equal to his passion for driving race cars.

I would like to express my gratitude to my co-writer, Joni B. Cole, whose editorial talents helped shape this book and make it a reality. From our first meeting to our last line edit, she made the writing process as enjoyable as it was meaningful.

I also had the pleasure of working with Nancy and John Grossman of Back Channel Press in Portsmouth, New Hampshire. Their sharp eyes, keen editorial instincts, and extensive knowledge about production made for a smooth transformation from manuscript to book.

For their many professional insights and encouragement, I extend my thanks and respect to Lynne Assad, PT, and Erika Villemure, PT, both of whom have devoted their careers to pelvic floor disorders. A special thanks goes to Talli Rosenbaum, MSc, PT, who has gone beyond the call to advise me about difficult problems and for her invaluable contribution to this book. My appreciation also extends to Elizabeth Stewart, MD, who stands as a beacon in the treatment of vulvovaginal disorders, and Lynne Margesson, MD, known internationally for her expertise in dermatologic disorders of the vulva.

For their willingness to share their expertise in sex counseling, I am grateful to Rhea Dyer, PhD; Paul Joannides, PsyD; Laurie Mintz, PhD; Gina Ogden, PhD; and Elke Reissing, PhD. Special thanks to Bat Sheva Marcus, PhD, who has devoted her career to women's disorders and is a maven in the treatment of low desire. And for her many insights and extensive hours of editing, a sincere thanks to Deborah Neel, PhD.

On a more personal note, I consider myself the luckiest father in the world to have the love of my three grown daughters, Debbie, Deenie, and Danielle. Added thanks goes to Danielle, the lawyer in the family, who in between bicycle racing with her husband, spent considerable time editing the manuscript, often after long hours in court defending her clients. My appreciation also extends to my wife's daughter, Nicole Piar, who created the cover art, interior illustrations, and design for this book. Her artistry is worth a thousand words in helping to tell the story of vaginismus.

And last, but hardly least, I would like to thank my wife, Janet, for her love, wisdom, strength, and companionship both at home and at work. Janet has contributed her many talents and expertise in graphic design, publishing, and marketing to our practice and outside projects. She is also my sweetie, my buddy, my cycling partner, my early-morning and late-night collaborator, and always the love of my life.

About the Author

Peter Pacik, MD, FACS, a recognized pioneer in treating patients with Botox for vaginismus, has been performing plastic surgery in Manchester, New Hampshire, since he completed his residency at SUNY Upstate Medical University in Syracuse, New York in 1972. He belongs to a small group of prestigious surgeons who are double board certified by both the American Board of Surgery and the American Board of Plastic Surgery. His practice has the honor of being the longest accredited surgi-center in the United States.

Dr. Pacik is the author of numerous scientific publications and is well known for his work on developing and researching pain control catheters used in breast enlargement surgery. He has been a long-time reviewer for the *Plastic and Reconstructive Surgery Journal, and the Aesthetic Surgery Journal,* and frequently presents scientific work at meetings and conferences. He is also a member of several organizations including the American Society of Plastic and Reconstructive Surgeons, American Society for Aesthetic Plastic Surgery, International Society of Clinical Plastic Surgeons, New England Society of Plastic and Reconstructive Surgeons, and the New Hampshire Medical Society. Dr. Pacik is a fellow of the American College of Surgeons.

Dr. Pacik is committed to furthering awareness about vaginismus through ongoing research, publications, speaking engagements, and interviews. For more info:

Peter T. Pacik, MD, FACS
Plastic Surgery Professional Association
57 Bay Street
Manchester, NH 03104

(800) 640-0290
info@plasticsurgerypa.com
http://www.plasticsurgerypa.com

About the Author

Joni B. Cole is an author, editor, and writing instructor. Library Journal "strongly recommended" her book *Toxic Feedback: Helping Writers Survive and Thrive;* and *American Book Review* stated, "I can't imagine a better guide to [writing's] rewards and perils than this fine book." Joni is also the creator of the acclaimed "This Day" book series, including *Water Cooler Diaries: Women Across America Share Their Day at Work.* Listed as "One of the Year's Notable Career Books" by the *New York Post,* the book was described as "both fascinating and eye-opening" by *Publisher's Weekly.* Joni is a frequent speaker at writing conferences, and has appeared on CNN and been a guest on numerous radio shows around the country. For more information: www.jonicole.com.

About the Illustrator

Nicole Piar is an illustrator and graphic designer who lives and works in a little house nestled in an Alder tree high above the big, crazy metropolis that is Los Angeles. She has designed and illustrated graphics for women's clothing, stationery, journals, notebooks, greeting cards, and gift products that are sold in stores such as Barnes and Noble, Macy's, Nordstrom, Michael's Arts and Crafts, and cute little speciality boutiques world-wide. She is currently writing and illustrating her first children's book. For more information: www.ghostkitten.com

About the Illustrations

The cover illustration depicts a woman enjoying her full luscious sensuality. She is at ease in her body and fearless in her sexuality. Women suffering from vaginismus often feel unfairly cut off from the sexual bliss that appears to come so effortlessly for some. The dark horizontal bands refer to this feeling of being barred off or separated from their own sexual fulfillment. The five black and white illustrations scattered across the book mark the journey of healing. A flower is the sexual organ of a plant. The slow blooming of the flower woman in the illustrations is a metaphor for emotional opening and blossoming sexuality.